Wake Up

& SMELL THE COFFEE

The Wake-Up Call You've Been Waiting For—Stop Following the Crowd, Start Following Your Heart.

Rebecca Hamilton

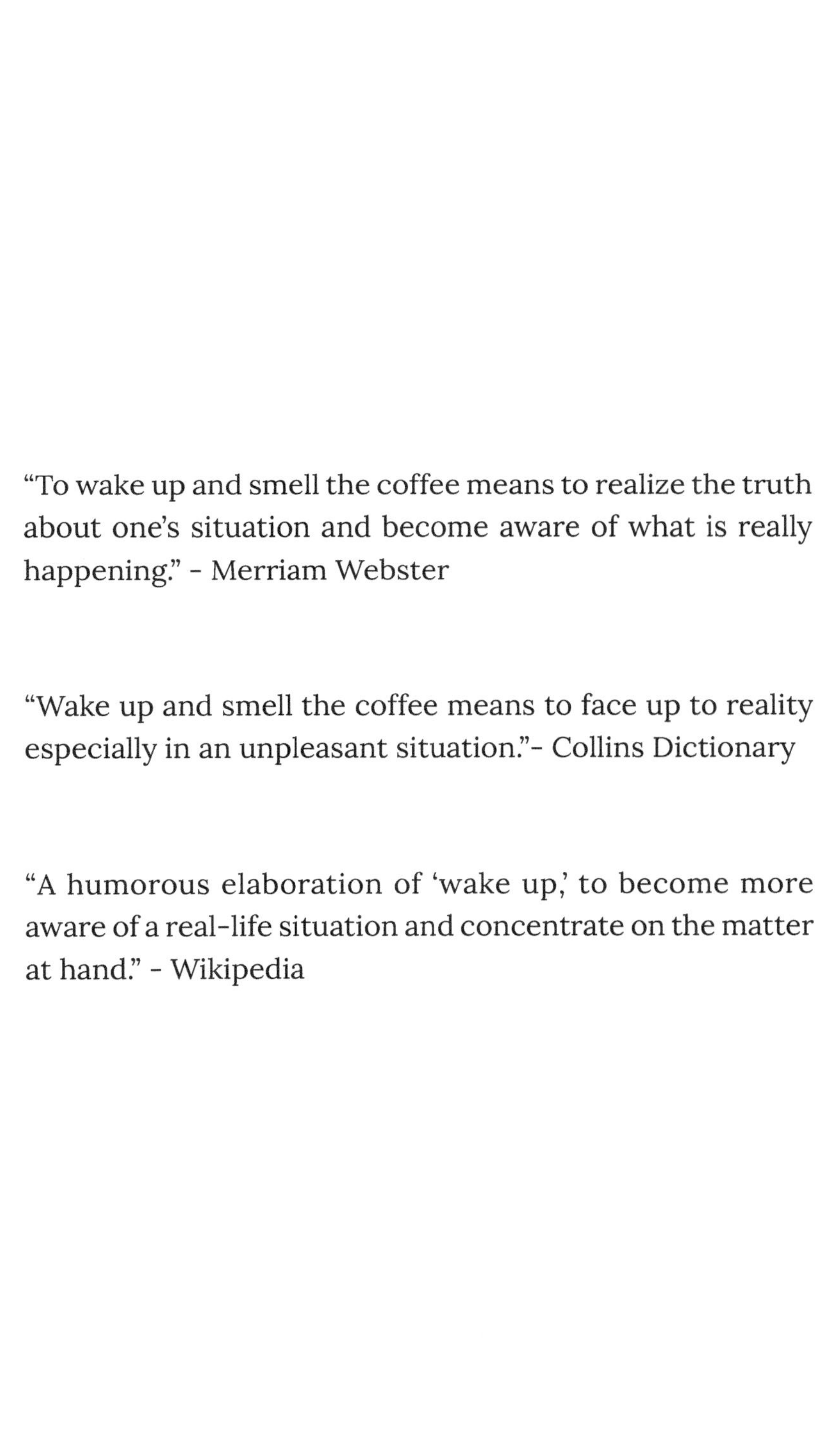

"To wake up and smell the coffee means to realize the truth about one's situation and become aware of what is really happening." - Merriam Webster

"Wake up and smell the coffee means to face up to reality especially in an unpleasant situation."- Collins Dictionary

"A humorous elaboration of 'wake up,' to become more aware of a real-life situation and concentrate on the matter at hand." - Wikipedia

At the heart of everything I do is a firm belief that connection is the key to a meaningful life. Real connection—with ourselves, each other, and the world around us—opens doors to new perspectives, deeper understandings, and a richer sense of purpose. I'd love to keep the conversation going and connect with you beyond these pages. Here's where you can join me:

- **Instagram:** @rebecca.hamilton.co

- **Podcast:** *Scrap the Sweet Talk*

- **Podcast Instagram:** @scrapthesweettalk

- **Website:** www.rebeccahamiltonco.com

DEDICATION

I dedicate this book to you, the reader—yes, you, the one holding this book and yearning for something deeper. You're not alone in feeling lost in a world that often prioritizes distraction over depth. I wrote this book to share all the indispensable lessons that I've learned in my life thus far that have guided me towards creating and living a deeply meaningful life amidst a numb, overindulgent, and unaware society.

We live in a world that is constantly vying for our attention, urging us to indulge in fleeting pleasures—social media scrolls, consumerist habits, and mindless eating—as a way to escape and cope with a stressful, shallow existence. I want to spark something within you, to help you see that there's so much more waiting beyond all the noise. May this book light a fire in your soul, empowering you to reclaim your power and courageously reshape your life to reflect your most authentic self.

You won't find any fancy credentials or capital letters strung together following my name like MD or PhD, and that's because I don't have any. I dropped out of high school at 16 to move out on my own after surviving a traumatic childhood. I battled through episodes of deep depression, crippling anxiety, periods of homelessness, and was on a dark trajectory to nowhere. Yet, from those struggles, I built a successful bakery from the ground up, reaching over a million dollars in revenue and publishing my first book, *The Million Dollar Bakery*.

I ran the bakery business with my husband for over a decade when, unexpectedly, life threw me a curveball: the very successful business I'd built became an agonizing source of conflict for me. Several years into running the bakery, I ended up embarking on my own health and wellness journey that resulted in me developing a significant disdain for sugar, processed foods, artificial flavours, food dyes, hustle culture, overindulging, vices, physical clutter and anything else that lacked intention and purpose in my life. This conflict of interest ended up leading to the closure of my beloved bakery business, which triggered an introspective inventory of everything that mattered and didn't matter to me.

After reading some influential books that further substantiated my feelings, I set out on an entirely new path that prioritized intentional living, authenticity, health, wellness, happiness, relationships, detachment, living in the present moment, and jettisoned literally everything else.

At first, it felt like I was swimming upstream in a modern culture that would do anything to retain my attention and drown me in all of its harmful habits required to cope in its distraught, zombie-like society. It didn't take me long to realize that without my own intervention to employ critical thinking skills or taking a step back to analyze the consequences of living how everyone else was, I'd inevitably end up just like them—miserable, unhappy, unhealthy and unfulfilled.

Why would I choose to proceed down a hopeless path led by people who were blindly following the crowd, living their lives at the mercy of external circumstances and at the expense of corporations that profit off their need to chronically self-soothe as a result?

The more aware I became, the more I realized that I had no choice but to forge my own path with the knowledge I'd been learning. At the end of this book, I will include a list of all the most influential books that have aided in my self-development journey thus far so that you have a list of resources to dive into after you've finished reading mine.

Everything I've shared in this book has been instrumental in my own journey, and I felt an undeniable calling to pass these lessons on to you. My hope is that you, too, can discover the profound transformation that comes from waking up each day, feeling fully alive, and taking the reins of your own destiny. It's time to step boldly into your own story, to embrace the uncertainty, and to chase your dreams with unwavering determination. Take what resonates with you, let it ignite your passion, and use it as fuel to create the life you've always envisioned.

Don't just read; act.

Don't just exist; thrive.

Your journey to a fulfilling, intentional life starts now, and I believe in you. Let your transformation begin!

CONTENTS

Introduction

Intentional

In·ten·tion·al (*adjective*): Done on purpose; deliberate.

You'll hear me use this word a lot in this book, so it's important that you understand its proper definition. Say goodbye to life as you know it, and allow me to welcome you to your new, *intentional* way of living. I'm so glad you're here!

Have you ever wondered why we have access to so much stuff and yet feel so empty? Or how we're technically more connected than ever through social media and yet feel so alone? Or why we work so hard and still feel broke, in debt, and like we're never going to get ahead? What about the fact that we're more medically advanced than at any other point in history, yet our entire population is more overweight, unhealthy, anxious, and depressed than ever before? I think you'd agree that something isn't adding up here...

Welcome to the rat race. Also known as the world's greatest shit show that we call—life. Where we're taught to sit down, shut up, and passively enjoy the show. Where we ravenously chuck hot buttered popcorn in the general direction of our mouths in a messy attempt at soothing our mundane misery. The plot of this show, which we call "Life," resembles the movie *Groundhog Day*, where we relive the same monotonous days over and over again—grinding, hustling, and consuming... starring us. The climax of the show is when we finally reach retirement (if you live long enough and don't die prematurely from chronic stress, of course). Ah, yes. This is the part of the show we've been looking forward to the most. It's the sole reason we've sacrificed the first 65 years of our lives on a hamster wheel—to hopefully end up at our "final destination," retirement. This is where we get to live the life we've always dreamed of. We finally get to do whatever the fuck we want. Except for one bleak and glaringly obvious thing...

The show is basically over. The end. Roll the credits. Cue the melancholic music.

Talk about a tearjerker... Or was it a psychological thriller because it left you feeling like "what the actual fuck?" Either way, I think we can all agree that when we look at our lives from a very literal perspective of what actually goes on in the absence of our own intentionality, it's nothing like what we envisioned it to be. There is no hope for a happy ending if we don't interject to realign our lives and intentionally redirect the plot toward a more purpose-filled, meaningful life—a life that we enjoy living daily and one that we would feel proud of by the end instead of burdened by.

We've been manipulated and conditioned to believe that if we trade 65 years of hard work, then we might, if we're lucky, get 20 years of so-called "freedom." That so-called freedom appears just in time for our minds to biologically decline and our bodies to begin deteriorating. Now, it doesn't take a whole lot of intellect to decipher the lack of mutual benefit in this trade. The dream of retirement is nothing more than a mirage of false hope to lure you through decades of hopeless days as it dangles a carrot on a stick that your dentures won't even be able to bite through by the time you're able to eat it. Retirement is the dream that one day, if you work hard enough, when you're significantly older and begin to physically and mentally deteriorate, you'll have an abundance of free time to do anything you want. When you retire, then you'll be free. Hip, hip (don't break a hip) hooray!

The only reason that society has marketed retirement as this magical destination to freedom is so that they can keep you stuck in a job and trapped in a lifestyle that perpetuates taxes and economic growth with no real regard for the meaning, depth, or quality of our lives at all.

The question we need to ask ourselves is why do we continue living our lives dictated by all these superficial societal beliefs when the value proposition is inadequate- the economy benefits while we personally suffer? This is the underlying truth that I want to share with you in this book. Think about it, if it weren't for society forcing you to believe that retirement is the answer to all your prayers and the pinnacle of "freedom," then surely you'd never instinctively choose to spend your life working so hard in a career you're bored with while prioritizing it over relationships, friends, family and hobbies.

...Would you?

I'm not saying we should all quit our jobs and hit the lam. Quite the opposite. Humans are meant to work, just not in the way society has conditioned us to interpret as the definition of "work". We've been led to believe that work should feel hard, long, tiring- gruelling even. Alas, we've been lied to in order for society to convince us to keep punching our time cards. What if I told you that work could feel fulfilling, purposeful, meaningful, exciting and, dare I say, fun? Humans have a natural inclination for work. In fact, we were meant to continue working indefinitely, not quit altogether once we reach a certain age at retirement. If the thought of working forever makes you cringe, then it's a clear sign you're in the wrong career. It's time to make a change. Who decided that work should feel like literal work? If you're not currently feeling a sense of purpose in your career, business, or life, then I'm so glad you picked up this book because it's going to help to redirect you to where you need to be.

The illusion of retirement was invented as a sort of backhanded reward for begrudgingly suffering through a mediocre career. I'm not debating whether we *should* work, but I'm asking you to redefine your *definition* of work and the purpose behind it. Think about back in the day when our ancestors would hunt for our food, build shelters, trade furs and textiles... That was work, and there was so much purpose in that type of work. It's work that helped humans to survive, evolve and that actually added value to each other's lives by trading essentials. Don't get me wrong, it's great that we've advanced to where we don't need to do those primal things in order to survive anymore, but we've taken it so far in the opposite direction that we've created this over-indulgent culture of consumerism, capitalism and materialism, resulting in the need to work more and trade our time for money so that we can buy an overabundance of useless things. Today, most of society is working at jobs that don't add meaning or purpose to their lives (or to the lives of others) and instead they're working at jobs that produce more products or services (many of which no one actually needs). I mean, just take a scroll through Amazon to see the overabundance of useless shit we're so eager to add to our carts. There are hundreds of variations of the exact same products out there. Do you really think that purchasing a different version of the same product is truly going to provide value to you? It's not. Since these products are not truly needed, the companies that make them are forced to heavily market and advertise them, desperately trying to make us believe they will enhance our lives. When they don't end up enhancing our lives how we'd been told that they would (because they never will), we reach for the next best thing and so on and so forth. We assume it's a problem with the thing itself when, really, it's a problem with our unhealthy attachment and desire for the thing. It's a never-ending cycle of overconsumption, buying into false promises, feeling let down and then desperately trying to fill the void of feeling let down.

Maybe you've never thought about your life like this. Most people haven't. That's exactly why our entire population is unhappier and unhealthier than ever before, despite significant advancements in our modern society. If it feels like you're having a moment of awakening that might feel like a raw slap upside the face, then good. Brace yourself, because this book is filled with plenty of harsh reality checks.

If we've never met before, you should know that I'm the type of friend who gives unbiased advice rooted in love, compassion and kindness, but without any kind of candy coating. I write all my books as if I were talking to someone I care about and though it wouldn't be my intention, I'm not afraid to offend you by speaking my truth. The more offended or triggered you get by something, the more truth it holds in your subconscious. If there wasn't any truth there, then it would've never sparked you to become offended or triggered in the first place. Triggers are our greatest teachers...but more on that later.

Sounds like the world and society are about to go to hell in a handbasket, doesn't it? The truth is, it might... but let's avoid being part of the shit show and stop inadvertently donating our lives to economic growth at the expense of our wellbeing. Let's be the different ones, the weird ones, the intentional ones, the authentic ones, the ones who lead by example and show the others what's possible. Let's be the change-makers.

I've spent the last decade of my life building my bakery business, Chick Boss Cake, from the ground up with no education or previous experience in business or in baking to over a million dollars in sales- grinding, hustling, consuming, repeat. I was a high school dropout who never in a billion years dreamed that I'd be capable of building a million dollar business. I have also written and published my first book, "The Million Dollar Bakery," about how I did it. Which again, was a major accomplishment for someone who only has a Grade 10 level English credit to her name. I had invested all my time, money and energy into my bakery business and it became the sole source of income for both my husband and I after he joined me in the business. It was on the up and up, sales increasing yearly and going so well. I had just won an award of excellence, being named London's Top 20 Under 40 for business achievement, professional expertise and community involvement. I had a loyal community full of support and really, no externally visible reason to not feel on top of the world. I felt so proud of my work ethic and accomplishments and yet, internally, a storm was brewing...

Several years into my business, I'd embarked on a significant health journey that resulted in me losing 70 lbs, cutting back on processed foods, quitting alcohol and decimating my refined sugar intake. Not to mention, I had developed a completely new mindset and way of living intentionally, minimalistically and deeply thanks to the teachings of The Minimalists, Eckhart Tolle, Arthur C. Brooks and Cal Newport (all exceptionally inspiring authors). This healthy lifestyle change was a complete 180° from the young, naïve, sugar-aholic, twenty-two-year-old who started her bakery business over a decade ago. I developed a healthy, much more intentional lifestyle that completely opposed my old desire for "bigger, better and more," which had been instilled in me and reinforced by society all these years.

So what does one do when they have worked so hard to build a successful business and life that ultimately no longer aligns with the person they've evolved into today?

Well, I guess I did what I felt like I *had* to do in order to realign and regain my sense of authenticity...

I quit.

In other words, I was forced to wake up and smell the coffee.

I found myself in a state of incapacitating incoherence. Perplexed by my own emotions and struggling with a serious case of cognitive dissonance, I was desperately trying to understand how on earth I ended up here. What brutal lesson was the Universe trying to teach me by leading me down a path of building a bakery business that had created so much success, only to later redirect me down an opposing path of health and wellness? It was unbelievable to me. Was it testing me to see if I'd continue to follow the original path in a blind desire solely for financial gain? Was it testing my ability to pivot and change in order to stay true to myself and live a thoroughly authentic life? Was it testing my resiliency for what felt like the millionth time in my life? I had no idea. All I knew was that it felt like a cruel, cruel joke.

Nevertheless, I was faced with a red pill vs blue pill situation. If you're unfamiliar with this analogy, so was I. I had heard it being discussed on a podcast that I was listening to although the idea originated from the movie *The Matrix*. Basically, you're presented with a choice between taking a red pill or a blue pill, with each pill providing different experiences. By choosing the red pill, it will make you learn a potentially unsettling truth, or by taking the blue pill, you remain oblivious to the truth and continue to live without the awareness that the red pill provides. Which pill would you choose? When I decided to embark on my health journey and learn about all the negative effects of sugar, processed foods, artificial dyes and flavourings, I was unknowingly swallowing the red pill. Now that I can't unlearn everything I'd learned, there was no going back. I had figuratively taken the red pill (perhaps in a few extra strength doses), and it was the point of no return for me. Admittedly, part of me wished I had picked the blue one and remained blissfully ignorant of these facts so that I could have continued with my lifestyle and business. However, I would be lying if I said I didn't feel like I was exactly where I was meant to be right now as a result of swallowing the truth.

Currently, I'm a few months into the new chapter of my life without my bakery business, and it already feels like my bakery business days were from another lifetime altogether. I look back at old photos and don't even recognize myself. Not a day goes by that I don't reflect on how grateful I am that I was brave enough to let go of a part of me that no longer aligned with the woman that I am today. Had I clung to that old identity, I would've cheated myself of my own authenticity.

In this book, I'll be sharing my personal journey of quitting my million dollar business and how I learned what it means to live an intentional, authentic, and meaningful life. I've spent a lot of time contemplating what we can do in order to create the life of our dreams *today*, despite all of our conditioning and preconceived beliefs that would like for us to believe that they're unreachable or, at best only attainable after we retire one day. I don't want to wait that long. Do you? How can we even be certain that we'll live that long?

I want you to create the life that you've fantasized about living in retirement right now. While you're as young as you'll ever be. I want you to feel so fulfilled daily and like it would be impossible for life to get better than it is in this present moment. Here's a little secret strategy that I learned to help get you started... It starts by *wanting* less which leads to *consuming* less, so that you can *work less* (but at a job you actually enjoy), so that you can ultimately *live more*. I promise that once you peel back the layers of all the false beliefs that society has tricked you into believing, you'll realize just how far down the wrong path you've been aimlessly wandering all these years. It's time to recalibrate that compass so that it points inward, not outward, and join me on a journey towards learning how to coexist harmoniously with an unconscious society while elevating your own consciousness.

Rest assured, I will not tell you to give up all the luxuries and material things you truly love. Love being a trick word here because as you'll learn in this book, you can't truly love material things at all (more about that in Chapter Seven). Instead, it's about changing our attachment to things that we *think* we love and understanding how to appreciate the functionality of them. It's about learning how to emotionally detach from material things and enjoy them for the objects that they are, and in doing so, you'll really begin to differentiate value from clutter. One of my favourite quotes is, "Love people and use things because the opposite never works," by The Minimalists. My goal with this book is to help you learn how to put the life back into the remaining years that you have left so that the rest of your life is filled with quality, not quantity.

It's easy to get frustrated, upset and to blame the world for brainwashing and molding us into the way that we are. After all, there is so much that we have to unlearn and many habits we have to break in order to live a happier life. It will require a significant amount of effort and accountability on our part before we see any progress. I agree it would be much easier if the world cared about our wellbeing and had our best interests at heart, but what if I told you that the problem isn't the world itself but instead, how we respond and choose to engage with it? Taylor said it best with the lyrics, "Hi, it's me. I'm the problem. It's me." Our mindless participation and lack of autonomy are the actual problems here. The best news of all is that if we are the problem, then we are also the solution. Instead of trying to force the world around us to change (an impossible feat), all we have to do is learn how to be intentional and change how we decide to engage and participate. What's equally as important is to choose how we will disengage. The outside world will continue to do what it needs to do in order to serve the economy, society, and maintain the status quo. Therefore, it is imperative that we take responsibility for our own best interests and do what we need to do in order to create a life that serves our soul's purpose and aligns with the most authentic versions of ourselves.

Like you, I've spent my entire life being heavily conditioned to live in a way that benefits society and consumerism. From the moment we entered the world, we've been told who we should aspire to be, what we should want, what we should have, how much money we should aim to make, what success looks like, what careers are worth pursuing, what level of education we should strive for, how big of a house we should live in, how nice of a car we should drive and as if that all doesn't sound cringy enough… The worst thing we've been taught is that if we decide to step outside this box that society has created for us, and choose to intentionally live a life that feels good despite all of that, we would be considered complete outcasts. You don't have the coolest clothes, latest phone, designer bag? As Gretchan would say, "You can't sit with us." The intense barrage of advertising, marketing and societal beliefs that are imposed upon us since birth is the sole reason that our society is unhappier, unhealthier, lonelier, and more hopeless than ever before. Our souls are being suffocated under the plethora of products, foods, vices and entertainment. All of which are being marketed to us, vying for our undivided attention and, most obviously, a spot on our credit card statements. They'll try to tell us it's going to "dramatically improve our lives," or better yet… "It'll make us happier," but I promise you… it's all being sold to us for the sole purpose of turning a profit. Our happiness and wellbeing is only as valuable to these companies as the money that we're willing to spend there.

You may have heard people proclaiming how they love living in a free country but, have you ever stepped back to ask yourself "how free are we really?" We *think* we live in a free country. We're *told* that we live in a free country. But the truth is that we'll never be truly free until we challenge our beliefs and ignite our own individual higher levels of awareness. I think that we all like the idea of living in a free country because it sounds wonderful, but I ask you to question how free do you really feel? I'm not talking about comparing your life circumstances and relative freedom to extreme examples of dictator-run communist countries, because I know some people (insert eye roll here) feel the need to justify and compare absolute worst-case scenarios to make themselves feel better in their own mediocrity. We're not going there right now, ok Linda? I think we can all agree that we are grateful for the level of comfort and safety we are privileged to have as a result of our geographic placement on this earth. However, let's remember that we can still feel grateful for things while simultaneously acknowledging major pitfalls in our culture and society (insert awareness and critical thinking development here). The first thing that we need to do is recognize that our freedom is being infringed upon by the beliefs society has been imposing on us to benefit the function of our economy and not our own personal well-being or happiness levels. In fact, the unhappier we are, the more we consume in attempts to fill the perpetual void with vices and material things. I'm going to teach you how I heightened my own level of awareness along with the dramatic life-changing effects that have resulted in creating a life that I'm *actually* excited to wake up to in the morning.

This book isn't about cultivating extreme points of view and living life in a state of protest or resistance—quite the opposite. This book is to help you expand your mind, gain consciousness and enhance your level of awareness so that you can choose to live a life that feels exciting, fulfilling and purposeful. It's time to realize that *we* get to decide how we participate in our modern society in a way that actually feels good instead of allowing society to continue sucking the life out of us.

One of the major topics we'll discuss in this book is our relationship to consumerism and our constant longing for "more." It's keeping us trapped. We end up sacrificing our most precious currency- time, in exchange for working our lives away, struggling to keep up with our insatiable desires for bigger, better, and more...bigger houses, better cars more stuff. Ugh, stuff. I hate the word stuff. The word itself makes me feel heavy, cluttered, bogged down and just plain uncomfortable. The definition of "stuff" is: "a person's belongings, equipment or baggage," baggage is right! The more stuff we accumulate, the more baggage we end up with, both physically and mentally. I'll be sharing all my tips on how to coexist in this material world without being completely consumed by it.

We're living in a world where people feel the need to identify themselves with some sort of "ist" in order to feel important- minimalist, perfectionist, feminist, activist...If you're looking for an "ist" that will actually serve you, then join me on the path to becoming an "intentionalist". Yes, I made that word up. As an "intentionalist" I intentionally choose to interrupt the thought process of the mindlessness associated with the excess of everything from overeating, overspending, overindulging, overworking, over-doing anything. I learned to only intentionally bring things into my life that add meaning or purpose to it. Notice that I didn't say that I stop the thought process and shut it out completely. I still have the thoughts. We are all human after all, but I am constantly interrupting those thoughts and challenging them as they arise to determine if they are intentional or not. Our sneaky little thoughts can often be caught trying to lure us into cheap indulgences that leave us feeling worse off if we give in to them with no true intention.

Along with challenging our thoughts and bringing awareness and intentionality to them, we must also mentally unsubscribe from the annoying, obnoxious marketing strategies of the world. Where companies pay millions of marketing dollars in attempts to convince us of what will or won't add meaning or purpose to our lives. As someone who quit alcohol as part of my health and wellness journey, I have to point out a very obvious example of the bias in marketing. Every single alcohol commercial I've ever seen highlights how happy and fun it appears to be as the carefree people pound back bottles around the campfire. I have never seen a Bud Light commercial that highlights the dark side of alcohol addiction, the numerous cancers associated with it, or the tragic consequences of drunk driving. Do you know why? Because the negative consequences aren't selling features (even though they're harsh realities of the ramifications of drinking). Imagine we lived in a world where companies had to share the good, the bad, and the ugly and let the consumer decide if their product was right for them after weighing out the pros and cons? Conveniently, the cons are always left out of marketing materials unless required by industry regulations to disclose (for example, smoking with the cancer risks on the boxes and prescription drug commercials that require the laundry list of side effects stated at the end of each commercial). Instead of blindly turning over our credit cards, what we actually need to do when it comes to buying into anything is... wait for it... engage our critical thinking skills, evaluate the pros and cons and decide for *ourselves* if we actually want or need something. Imagine that. We can do this, guys!

Just like you, I got coaxed into the propaganda of working hard, hustling, grinding, wanting more things, making tons of money, spending tons of money and trying to relentlessly level up my hustle game in hopes that it would continue to match my exceeding desires for bigger and better. By the way, the definition of propaganda according to the Oxford Dictionary is: "Information, especially of a biased or misleading nature, used to promote or publicize a particular political cause or point of view." If you search synonyms for propaganda, the words: "advertising, promotion and publicity" show up. In other words, advertising, which is also known as marketing, is in fact propaganda- the biased or misleading nature used to promote or publicize a particular point of view. Keep that top of mind next time you're scrolling through social media being bombarded with ads for products of the utmost uselessness vying for your attention and unrequited access to your wallet. How did we ever convince an entire population to work their lives away and trade their most valuable asset (time) just so they could afford to accumulate more "stuff" that eventually someone else will either inherit or be burdened to throw away after they die? Look at all of the things in and around your own home and see all the objects, knickknacks, accent furnishings, and all the other material things that you've traded your time for over the years. You put in hours upon hours at work to be able to afford to purchase these things. Just so that it can sit there. If you're anything like me, go peek inside your closet. I am guilty as charged. I enjoy pretty clothing. It's not wrong to have things that you value and enjoy, but the question is- how much of it do we *actually* value and enjoy? I know for me, it's nowhere near 100% of it. How much less would you have to work if you didn't keep adding to your collection of things?

For God's sake, you guys. This is a trap. Wake up! Your life is happening right now, in the present moment. It doesn't just magically start one day when (and if) you make it to your 65th birthday so that you can finally retire and live the life of your geriatric dreams. The idea that you're willing to trade the present moment, aka the only moment that you literally have, in hopes that one day in the faraway future (when you're closer to biological death), you can do what you actually want to do… is insane.

It's fucking insane, you guys!

The good news is that you picked up this book, and together we're going to get you well on your way to living your best life in the present moment. Every. Single. Day. We're setting you up so that there is nothing better, happier, or more fulfilling than the life you're living today. We don't need to look forward to something. The future doesn't even exist. Let me ask you, if you started living the "retirement" fantasy you've created in your mind today, then what would you be working so hard towards? Nothing. You would be working at a reasonable pace while prioritizing the things that matter most to you, at a job that allows you to utilize your natural skills that feels impactful and serves others and then you'd come home to a life you've intentionally created that feels peaceful, aligned and authentic to you. You would find out what true happiness feels like and learn to enjoy the present moment for what it is. While it's nice to have hopes, dreams and goals for the future, we waste far too much time in our heads planning and far too little time in our hearts simply *enjoying*. We've all heard the figurative philosophy of "what if you died tomorrow?" and yet, we dismiss the deeper meaning and resist the inevitability behind it. I ask you to contemplate this question from a literal standpoint...

What if you did indeed die tomorrow?

I'll tell you what. Your unlived hopes and dreams will die with you. Retirement most definitely won't matter now that you're dead, and if there is hindsight in death, you'd wish that you lived every day actively pursuing your purpose and living an intentional, authentic and meaningful life true to yourself. No one would die feeling proud that they sacrificed quality time with family and friends because they worked so hard at a job that made them miserable simply so that they could afford a bigger house and fill their voids with Chanel bags. Both of which, the house and Chanel Bags, no longer physically belong to you now that you're dead. Some other random family will buy and live in your house and some randos will thrift your coveted Chanel bags. What's more important? Leaving behind a whack-load of lacklustre things that provided cheap entertainment for a miniscule amount of time? Or leaving behind fewer objects and things and instead leaving a group of people you loved who were deeply inspired and impacted by your presence in their lives? The answer to this question lies in the choices that you make every day.

What are the consequences if we don't wake up, smell the coffee and start living intentionally?

Well, the evidence is clear. Take a look around at the result of this capitalistic, overindulgent, brainwashed culture that's been cultivated to prioritize economic growth and subsequently created a society that's more depressed, lonely, unhappy, tired, anxious, unhealthy, suicidal and addicted than ever before. No wonder mental illness, chronic stress, and addictions are at an all-time high. We're being stripped of our human-ness and natural desires, being rewired to work forty plus hours a week at a job that, statistically speaking, most people hate, for most of our lives all for the purpose of buying and accumulating more useless stuff.

We've been forced to desperately find ways to numb, cope and comfort ourselves amid these unrealistic and unnatural demands that've been imposed upon us and it's killing us. It's quite literally killing us. It's killing us mentally, emotionally, physically and spiritually. It's no wonder we've created a cultural norm of overindulging in the excess of alcohol, shopping, drugs and food, in a desperate feeble attempt to cling onto any amount of shallow joy to soothe our tired, overworked bodies and souls. I need to ask you, what about this sounds appealing? Nothing, I hope, now that I've painted such a grim ultra-realistic picture for you. There should be no legitimate reason to continue carrying on like this for one minute longer. Make this commitment to yourself starting today. I made the decision to listen to my heart and accept the reality that I had outgrown my old life. I had become a healthier, happier and a much more intentional woman and if closing my business was the price I had to pay to fully honour and embrace her, I'd pay it ten times over again. There's no greater quote that comes to mind than this one, "Your new life is going to cost you your old one," by Brianna Wiest.

And so it began... my love affair with life. I became so passionate about feeling alive, engaged and fully present that anything that *didn't* make me feel that way... had to go. I guess you could say that I "Marie Kondo'd my soul" and categorized things in my life into piles of what sparked joy and what didn't. Then, I unapologetically allowed myself to declutter my spirit. I challenged my old ways of being that I'd been previously conditioned to believe that no longer served me on a soul level. I began to think about our evolution as a human species and I categorized all my conditioned beliefs and activities into the two following categories:

1. **Human nature ways of being**: characteristics and habits that have been genetically wired into us naturally from the beginning of time. Think about things like being in nature, eating whole foods, moving our bodies, prioritizing relationships, connecting with our communities and the contentment of living our lives in the present moment.

2. **Man-made ways of being**: characteristics and habits that have been created by humans artificially to serve our society, economy, and the material world. Think about things

like consumerism, processed foods, working hard to be able to afford more stuff, capitalism, social media, overvaluation of money, constant comparison to others and being obsessed with wanting more.

Again, evolution and man-made things aren't the enemy here. The problem is our own lack of discipline in the overindulgence of superficial man-made habits and characteristics. No one is throwing down millions of dollars in marketing campaigns to promote the "human nature way" of being because it cannot be sold. It's our own responsibility to be aware of this and choose to align our lives accordingly. Someone who is completely entangled in the man-made mentality might choose to work upwards of 80 hours a week just so that they can afford to buy their dream car, only to discover that when the novelty wears off (and it always does) they're not as happy as they'd anticipated. This is because they're overestimating the ability of man-made objects to provide lasting happiness. Our culture relies on this idealization in order to maintain economic precedence. Meanwhile, in many Eastern cultures where they prioritize human nature, you'll see communities that appear to have less material things but possess more joy, fulfilment, peace, and ultimately, true lasting happiness. I encourage you to research: "The Blue Zones" of the world. These are areas in the world where people live the healthiest and longest lives. We could learn a thing or two (or fifty) from them.

I'll be the first to admit, it took *a lot* of convincing for me to even be open to the idea that my conditioned beliefs were not serving me. I didn't work hard to build a million dollar business because I didn't care about material things. I totally thought that anyone who wasn't actively hustling, grinding, and consuming had just given up on life and admitted defeat. I believed they were taking the easy (or lazy) way out. It's easy not to challenge our societal beliefs when everyone else is carrying on as if misery is supposed to be normal. It wasn't until I asked myself if the results I was witnessing from myself (and everyone else around me who was also living like this) looked in any way appealing to me. Work hard, buy stuff, retire, get rid of stuff, die. It didn't take me long to come to my conclusion, which was:

Abso-fucking-lutely not.

When we learn to live in a way where we prioritize human nature and make man-made things less of a priority, then we can get back to our roots and experience what it really means to be human. This is the only opportunity that we have to tap into true happiness. It's not to say that we shouldn't enjoy made-made things or that we should feel guilty for doing so, but if we rearrange our lives to prioritize human nature first, many of the other things will inherently begin to matter less.

It's time.

Time to grab your favourite mug or tumbler (don't lie we all have one), fill it with your preferred hot, cozy beverage (I won't be offended if it's not coffee, I'll just assume you're weird), and let me share with you the most soul-awakening book that I've had the privilege of writing for you. I like to write my books in the same context as how I talk in real life to my friends- comfy, casual, witty, lots of weird puns, quotes, stupid lyrics and naturally, a few swear words for dramatic effect. Haven't you heard the saying that you should never trust someone who doesn't swear? I'm *very* trustworthy.

This book is for all the small business owners and entrepreneurs who work their asses off in a society that glorifies hustle, hard work, grinding and makes it feel impossible to get ahead otherwise...

It's for all the doctors, nurses, lawyers, officers, firefighters, and CEOs who've built their entire identity around their careers so strongly that they no longer know who they really are outside of their occupations...

It's for the ones who are working hard, saving all their money and fantasizing about retirement in order to be able to finally get to do all the things they've always dreamt of doing...

It's for the people who feel like being "so busy" is something to be proud of and who wear it as a badge of honour...

It's for the people who are feeling uninspired, unhappy, or unfulfilled...

It's for the ones who are trudging through life on autopilot, unaware and unconscious of everything around them...

It's for the ones who are depressed about the past, feeling like the good old days are far behind them....

It's for the ones who are anxious about the future, hoping for brighter days ahead...

It's for you—the one who is currently living life within the limited confines of our preconceived and heavily conditioned societal beliefs that have been imposed upon us since birth…

It's time to wake up, and smell the coffee.

Chapter One

CE-OVER IT—WHEN TO QUIT

The fluorescent lights burned as I painfully opened one eye, squinting and wincing as the artificial brightness felt like a laser beam piercing a hole straight through my head. I grudgingly brought my elbow up to my face to shield myself from its horrendous intensity and pulled the blanket up and over my head.

I shuffled from my left side to my right side and then back and forth a few more times in a desperate attempt to fall back asleep. Ugh. I'd give anything just to fall back asleep. My head was pounding with the most painful tingling sensations. I'd never experienced anything like it. It felt like hundreds of tiny snakes were slithering around the inside of my head, aggressively gnawing away at the interior of my skull. The light from the ceiling was obnoxiously bright as it shined through the thin fibers of the hospital blanket, somehow still penetrating through my firmly shut eyelids. It was useless. I was awake, and so were my pain receptors. With my eyes closed and the blanket still covering my face, I thrashed my arm around haphazardly in a blind search for the little red button. With wires protruding from my arm, tangling more with every flail, I finally located the little button that had fallen between the crevasse of the mattress and the bed railing. My fingers pulsed the button erratically as a nurse came bolting into the room.

"More medication, please," I mumbled from under the covers.

She sat me up and peeled the sweat-laden blanket off my flushed red face and cheerfully said, "Good morning," as she energetically opened the curtains, causing the stark white walls to glow with more bright, irritating light.

Still clenching my eyes shut in an attempt to delay the burning from the bright lights, I repeated my painful plea for more medication, to which she insisted on taking my vitals for what felt like the 800th time since I was admitted to the ICU. *Clearly, my vitals were fine if I was still breathing and feeling pain, I thought to myself.* I could feel my pulse pounding through my brain, so I knew it was still there.

With no energy to argue, I obliged with the routine vital check, hoping it would mean being administered more pain meds sooner rather than later. Besides checking my vitals, they also took my blood work daily, sometimes twice a day. Not only did I have an extreme aversion to needles, but I just so happened to have been blessed with the type of veins that are impossible to find on a good day. My arm was already fifty shades of deep blue and purple, covered in bruises due to the many previous attempts at locating my veins, and each time it took more pokes and prods to finally collect enough blood for testing.

Squeamishly, I turned my arm over to the nurse as she applied pressure to my throbbing, bruised skin. I clenched my jaw in anticipation as I braced myself for the sting of the needle plunging into my raw, tender skin. When having blood drawn, the more tension you create, the more pain you experience...but I couldn't help it.

After the nurses finished their routine checks, I finally received my dose of pain medication—Dilaudid. Injected via yet another needle, except this one was going in my leg, not the bruised arm. The pain of its administration was excruciating, a searing rush that felt like shards of fragmented glass slicing through my insides. My skin felt like it was literally crawling. I sank back into my soggy bed that was still damp from profusely sweating throughout the night and desperately tried to find a moment of peace. My gaze fixed on the clock on the wall, its relentless ticking grating on my nerves. Time dragged on as I waited, desperately hoping for the Dilaudid to get rid of the suffocating pain that consumed me.

Next thing I knew, I awoke to the dull sound of incessant beeping. I quickly realized it was just the hospital machines, and eventually, they became background noise to a hectic conversation I was overhearing in the hallway right outside my room. Two police officers were there, taking statements from the nurses. I heard one of them say:

"He's been arrested for assault after attempting to break into the hospital after visitor hours and threw a needle at the nurse. I'll play back the surveillance footage to determine if any further charges will be brought forth, but for now, he's being detained at our station until further notice.

I'm not sure if anyone has let Rebecca know yet or if we should just let her sleep. I'll let you guys make that call."

My mind spun wildly, heart pounding as I lay there, holding my breath, clinging to their every word. The sound of the surveillance footage filled the space—play, pause, rewind—an erratic, jarring sequence that mirrored the chaos unfolding. Each replay sent a fresh wave of anxiety through me.

I heard who I assumed was one of the police officers pause the video and say, "Yep. You can see right here where he picks up the needle and aggressively hurls it toward the nurse on duty. That's going to result in aggravated assault charges, and he's going to end up getting a lengthy sentence for this. That's all I needed to see."

He continued, "I'll need a copy of this footage sent to the investigation unit at our department immediately. Thank you for your time and cooperation. We will be on our way now."

I started feeling sick to my stomach. They were talking about my husband, Chad. This didn't sound like him at all. I'd known him for over ten years and had never seen anything close to an aggressive side. The angriest I'd ever seen him was when the Montreal Canadiens lost in the playoffs. He had a healthy range of emotions, but anger and aggression were not one of them.

I guess any human has the capability to snap under immense pressure, and I'm sure if it came down to it, he'd do whatever he felt he had to in order to see me, I thought to myself. But what the hell was he thinking? I was so mad at him. I was lying sick in the hospital, and he was the one responsible for running our business. My mind raced, wondering what would happen now—with me so ill and him locked up. This was the last thing I needed to worry about.

Bound to my hospital bed by wires and tubes, feeling panicked and helpless, I reached for my phone. Obviously, I couldn't call or text Chad since he was in jail, so I texted my mom instead. My message was something like, *Chad got arrested for throwing a needle at a nurse, and he's in jail. I'm still in the hospital, and I don't know what to do.*

She called me immediately, saying she was leaving work and would be on her way. I was too weak and groggy from the medication to do anything else, and eventually, I passed out.

I woke up in a heavily medicated daze to the sound of my mom's voice in the room. She was talking to the nurses in charge of my care, inquiring about the dose of Dilaudid I was on. My mom, being a registered nurse, understood the gravity of the situation and didn't seem impressed at all that I was being administered a drug four to eight times stronger than morphine.

The nurses assured her they had already tried other pain relievers and that nothing else was working.

As I slowly came to, my mom asked, "How are you feeling?"

"Not good," I replied. "How long is Chad in jail for?"

An unimpressed smirk crossed her face. It was the kind of look you receive from your mother as a child when you did something wrong—it shouldn't be funny, but it is, and they don't know whether to laugh or cry about it. That's the look I got.

She sat on the edge of my bed and said, "Chad is fine. Everything is fine. No one is in jail. You can call him; he's just not allowed to visit right now because you're only permitted one visitor per day, per hospital regulations. But I've already talked to him."

Confused and disoriented, I racked my tired brain, struggling to piece together what was happening. "Ok, so they let him out of jail then? I don't understand. Why did he throw a needle at the nurse?" I asked.

"Honey, none of that happened. It's okay. The medication they have you on is very strong, and I've told the nurses to lower your dose because it's causing you to hallucinate."

I sat there, stunned and skeptical, wondering if she was lying to keep me calm and relaxed. "No, it definitely happened. I was here. I heard everything clear as day. I need to call him."

By this point, I'd been in the intensive care unit for three days, and there was no doubt that the drugs were building up in my system. They still didn't know what was wrong with me aside from my obvious symptoms: fever, vomiting, excruciating head pain, and chills. They suspected meningitis and had performed a couple of spinal taps (I'll spare you the details). Now, we were awaiting the results to see if it was bacterial, which can be life-threatening, or viral, which makes you very sick but has a high recovery rate.

Still convinced that everything I'd witnessed that morning had actually happened, I called Chad to find out his side of the story.

"Are you in jail? I'm so mad at you! Why would you think it's okay to throw a needle at a nurse? The poor woman is just trying to do her job. Who is going to run our business with me chained to this hospital bed and you in jail?" I dramatically asked.

"Babe, babe, babe!" He tried to interrupt me several times during my delusional interrogation. "Everything is fine. I'm fine, the nurses are fine. I'm not sure what you thought you heard or saw this morning when you woke up, but none of that actually happened."

"Huh? I'm so confused," I replied.

"The painkiller you're on is causing side effects of delusion and hallucinations. I've been talking to the doctor at the hospital about it, and he said that though it's rare, it's not completely uncommon to have that happen as a result of high doses of Dilaudid. They're going to be lessening the dose, but in the meantime, everything is fine. The business is under control, and your mom is going to stay here with you for today. I love you, and I'll call back later to check in."

Part of me still didn't believe it. I thought for sure that he and my mom were just trying to tell me what I needed to hear in order to keep me calm. I sat there the rest of the day, continuing to see and hear strange things appearing throughout my hospital room. There were cartoon characters on the walls and all kinds of colourful shapes appearing and disappearing. At one point, I became infuriated and asked the nurse if the hospital could stop playing Disney music over their PA system because the voices of Timon and Pumbaa singing *Hakuna Matata* were driving me absolutely nuts. The nurses were so patient and kind, going along with my false sense of reality to help keep me relaxed and comfortable.

As the evening descended like a heavy curtain, the moment arrived for my mom to leave, plunging me into a whirlwind of intense hallucinations. The instant she stepped out, and I found myself alone in that sterile room, the world around me transformed into a nightmarish landscape. Vivid voices erupted from the shadows, echoing with a terrifying urgency. I heard a chaotic stampede of authorities barrelling down the hall, their footsteps pounding like the beat of a heart. They dragged the head doctor into an empty ICU room, their voices sharp and frantic.

"If we don't evacuate the patients from the hospital immediately, this entire place is going to explode and burn to the ground! When it does, you will be held legally responsible for every soul that perishes. The electrical wiring has been compromised, and we don't have a moment to lose!"

I heard them arguing back and forth, and the head doctor replied, "This hospital can't afford to close down. We are not evacuating. We need to keep the patients in their rooms and continue to operate business as usual. Do not alert the patients!"

"Holy fuck," I thought to myself as I began frantically un-clipping and unplugging all the wires attached to me. I remember wrapping my hospital gown tighter around my waist to ensure it adequately covered my butt as I got ready to bolt. The only thing I couldn't get off was the IV that was securely taped to my arm, so I just grabbed the whole IV unit and started to bee-line out of my ICU room.

A nurse ran after me, asking where I was going so abruptly. "Don't pretend like you don't know what's going on here. I heard everything!" I declared with absolute confidence. "This place is going to explode any minute!"

As the nurse gathered her thoughts and maintained ab-solute composure, she gently wrapped her arm around me. With an unsettling serenity in her voice, she leaned in close and whispered, "No, honey, you're safe, and everything is fine. That is not going to happen."

I blankly stared at her, feeling like I was in a horror movie where the killer patronizingly assures the victim that there's nothing to worry about in the most eerily calm manner before they massacre their prey. I couldn't tell if she was being genuine or condescending or if she was "in" on the so-called plan for the hospital to explode.

As she talked me back into my room and re-hooked me up to all the machines, someone reached out to my emergency contact, which was my husband, Chad, to see if he could help calm me down. I demanded that he come to the hos-pital immediately, despite it being past visitor hours and having already had my mom there earlier, who was the one visitor I was allowed that day. The hospital staff made an exception and allowed him to come—probably partially for their own sanity. Nevertheless, I was very thankful.

Chad rushed to the hospital with frantic urgency, but by the time he arrived, I had already spiralled into a vortex of terrifying, nightmarish hallucinations that consumed the remainder of the evening. The hospital staff, witnessing my descent into madness, granted him permission to stay overnight. He settled onto the cold, sterile floor beside my bed, cocooned in a thin blanket. If that's not true love, I don't know what is.

In the dead of night, I was yanked into a horrifying nightmare so disturbingly vivid that it jolted me awake, and I exploded into a blood-curdling scream. A flurry of nurses burst into the room, their expressions etched with alarm as they rushed to uncover the source of my terror. After that moment, everything slipped into a hazy void. I can only assume that they administered a powerful sedative, lulling me back into a deep sleep.

My creative imagination had never done me so dirty before. Usually, my creativity is my greatest gift, allowing me to photograph, paint, write, and create magic. But evidently, it was a different story when tripping out on hard opioid drugs. I think my lack of experience with drugs, paired with my creative imagination and the strength of the Dilaudid, created the perfect storm of hallucinations. To this day, I can remember them as if they were absolutely 100% real, and I can't believe that something that felt so real... wasn't. It completely blew my mind.

When my test results finally came back clear of any bacterial infection, the doctors concluded I had viral meningitis (the non-deadly kind), and discharged me. This hospital stint lasted six days in the ICU, followed by another two months at home as I struggled to regain my strength and appetite. To this day, I still don't know how I came down with meningitis, but it was by far the sickest I'd ever been in my life. The illness and the medications had drained my strength; I struggled to walk to the end of my street without feeling utterly exhausted and gasping for air. Unable to keep food down, my diet was reduced to Boost nutritional supplement drinks (which, it turns out, are not as nutritious as they claim but ended up doing the job), along with lots of rest.

Not only was this a difficult time for me, but my husband was traumatized by the entire ordeal, too. As soon as the doctors speculated I had meningitis, he did what no one should ever do (but always does anyway) and Googled the diagnosis. In classic Google fashion, the worst-case scenario popped up first, stating that it could be potentially fatal. Pair that with my delusional behaviour, and it was distressing for him, to say the least.

I remember coming home from the hospital. We pulled our Jeep into the driveway just as we had done countless times before, and I couldn't help but wonder: how many people who go to the hospital never get to return home? They exit their home for the last time. Never to experience walking through their own front door, ever again. Every other time I came home from an outing, I would instinctively pull into the driveway, turn off the car, gather my things, and step out without a second thought—except for the rare moment when I'd mentally note the yard work that needed to be done. Yet what once seemed like a mundane routine suddenly took on profound significance. The thought that everyone, at some point, experiences leaving their home for the very last time was jarring. Before this realization, I guess I'd just assumed that my home would always be... *my home*. That's just what we do, isn't it? We assume we're going to live forever and that all of our things will always be... *our things*. The undeniable reality is that there's a last time for everything: coming home, visiting your grandparents, seeing your mom's name on the call display, walking through the halls of your old school, and eating a family dinner with everyone at the same table. It was in this realization that I came to terms with the fact that we don't actually own our homes. In fact, we don't actually own anything. In most cases, our things end up owning us.

This was a pivotal moment of realization for me because I had previously been the typical girl who loved all of my possessions, and my home was no exception. As an introvert, my home was actually at the top of the list of my most cherished belongings. I had poured so much love and attention into renovating and personalizing it over the years, and it was where I enjoyed spending the majority of my time. It took me a good few months to come to terms with the grim, depressing reality that my home wasn't truly mine. I began picturing someone else buying it when I died, taking possession of all my beloved belongings. From that moment on, I realized I had no choice but to accept this harsh truth. I couldn't pretend that it wouldn't happen one day, yet the thought made me excruciatingly uncomfortable.

Then, something came to me out of the blue. I'm not sure if you've ever experienced this, but it felt as though the Universe sent me a download of information, seemingly out of nowhere, to help guide me on my journey. Suddenly, I knew what I needed to do: I had to learn how to detach my sense of self from my personal belongings and cherished possessions. It was the only way forward... but how?

I'll be sharing my personal journey of detachment and how I learned to develop a healthy appreciation for my material things without tying my identity to them or attaching my self-worth to them. More on detachment in Chapter Seven.

In the meantime, take a moment to reflect on all of your favourite things. What objects or material possessions do you love, value, or think you would struggle to let go of? This question is worth considering before we dive deeper into this topic later on.

Oh, and don't worry... as I mentioned earlier, I'm not suggesting that we get rid of all our meaningful possessions. I'm simply going to teach you how to change your relationship and attachments to them. By doing this, I've learned to appreciate my material things in a whole new way while also finding peace in the understanding that I do not own a single thing in this world—and neither do you. Everything is simply borrowed.

Are bouts of sickness signs of divine intervention? Are they a manifestation of our unconscious minds creating resistance that forces us to rest, reflect, and redirect our paths? Or are they completely random? This thought crossed my mind, and truthfully, I still have no idea. I don't think any of us know the real answer to this, but the timing of my illness was peculiar, to say the least. Just a couple of weeks before my admittance to the hospital, I had signed a lease for a new bakery location that we were about to start setting up. Part of me was furious that my illness struck at such an inopportune time, while the other part wondered if it was a wake-up call from the Universe, signalling that it was time to move on from this business. Unfortunately, if it was a wake-up call, I wasn't ready to answer it—I sent that bitch straight to voicemail.

Ignoring my better judgment, I dove back into work the only way I knew how: at full speed. I didn't have time to heed this message from the Universe. Who did it think it was, interrupting my tight schedule? There was so much to accomplish, and I had even less time and energy to get the new location up and running before the rent payments started draining from my account. Rent didn't care if we were ready or not.

Despite feeling tired and weak after my recent hospital release, I dove back into work, determined to put forth my best effort in setting up the new store location. What was I supposed to do—take a time-out? Step back? Rest? Recover? Reflect on whether I should continue growing this wildly successful business that I had worked so hard to build from the ground up? Who had time for any of that? Certainly not me. It seemed like a no-brainer to keep barrelling through, and that's exactly what I did as I opened my fourth bakery location just a couple of months later.

As they say, hindsight is always 20/20—clear as day. There were many signs before I got sick trying to steer me in a new direction, and many more afterwards. The warning signs didn't stop coming until I started to really pay attention to them. In my experience, the Universe will continue throwing signs your way until you actually stop to notice and start heeding them. Generally, they begin subtly—like a couple of soft nudges—but if you ignore them for long enough, it's only a matter of time before they escalate into a full-blown punch in the face. The goal is to tune in and see the signs before they get to that point. I'm usually good at following signs and redirecting my path, but my business presented a classic battle between head and heart. Logically, my head urged me to continue, given how far I'd come and the effort I'd invested. However, my heart had left long before—well before my health journey and aversion to sugar. It departed when I stopped pursuing my passion for crafting aesthetically pleasing desserts and instead appointed myself as the CEO.

As my business grew to meet increasing demands, I felt I had to hang up my apron and step into the role of CEO. Some might see this as a promotion, but I didn't start my bakery business because I longed for a corner office with a view. Building a business from the ground up to over a million dollars is often seen as a success, and many believe that the goal is to work on the business rather than in it. I thought this transition would be straightforward—after all, how hard could it be? It turns out that it was pretty freaking hard and exceptionally soul-crushing to my little artist heart. The artistic expression I cherished took a backseat, making this role misaligned with my purpose and passion. I've seen many small business owners fall into the same traps, ultimately losing both their businesses and their sense of self in the process. I feel a deep sense of responsibility to share the key differences between small business owners and CEOs in order to help you stay on the right track in your business or career. Too often, I see people accepting promotions solely for the increase in pay or due to feeling pressured to do so, instead of asking themselves if the new position is aligned with their gifts. It's a big mistake. Let's explore the differences between small business owners and CEOs below. If you're an employee working for someone else, the underlying message still applies—don't accept a promotion unless the job duties are something that will light you up every single day.

Small Business Owners

Small business owners usually have worked really hard to build and grow their business from the ground up and have forged a way to turn their passion/hobby into a business. They pour their hearts and souls into their product or service and are commonly found working *in* their business. Their passion is closely tied to the creation of the product or the skill of the service. For many small business owners, assuming roles in their own companies that are not directly tied to their gifts and strengths is a recipe for disaster. Usually, a small business starts with someone who has pursued a passion of some kind and decided that they wanted to make a business out of it so that they could make a career out of something they're passionate about. This can be extremely fulfilling if you execute it properly and set the appropriate boundaries for yourself so that you don't get sucked into the chaos of wearing all the hats and trying to juggle all the departments on your own. The problem is, as soon as you turn a passion into a business, you're suddenly responsible for the business duties too (hiring and HR, bookkeeping, payroll, marketing, advertising, processes, customer service just to name a few). These business related duties eventually end up taking more and more time away from the very thing that sparked the passion for you to start the business in the first place. If you're a small business owner or considering becoming one, I cannot stress the importance of sticking with your gift and strength within your business and hiring out the rest. When we cross over into areas that aren't our strengths, it ends up sucking the life and passion right out of us (and our business), leading to burnout, fatigue, unfulfilment and just plain misery.

<u>CEOs</u>

In contrast, CEOs are positioned to work *on* the business rather than *in* it, and they thrive in managing daily operations. Their skills are adaptable across various industries, allowing them to apply standardized business knowledge effectively. The movement to shift small business owners out of daily operations and into a more traditional CEO role is gaining traction. While this shift may seem like sound business advice, it's essential to remember what initially fuelled the passion for the business.

For instance, if you are a hairstylist who loves cutting and styling hair, transitioning into a CEO role filled with administrative tasks may lead to discontentment. A better approach might be to remain focused on your passion while partnering with someone whose strengths complement yours, allowing you to delegate the oversight and management duties.

Not every small business needs a CEO; many could thrive with a General Manager instead. I've noticed a trend where small business owners are eager to adopt the CEO title without considering whether their business is structured to support it. If a business cannot afford to pay a competitive CEO salary, it might be wise to prioritize other aspects before seeking a title that may not align with the company's size or needs.

Another thing I feel compelled to point out is that we can be blinded by the prestige and allure of certain job titles. Our society does an excellent job at perpetuating this by glorifying success based on position rather than the value of the work itself, often leading individuals to chase titles instead of true fulfillment. Regardless of whether you're a small business owner, a CEO, or an employee, linking your identity to a job title can be very problematic. While seeking validation from your career is a common human impulse, it's vital to cultivate self-worth from within. You don't need additional letters or titles to validate your worth; your significance comes from who you are, not from your job title.

For the longest time, I never felt the need to change or modify my job title. "Owner" had always worked just fine—or as my regular customers affectionately dubbed me, "the blue-haired cake lady." The thought of adding those three capital letters to my title filled me with hesitation. Was I really qualified to be a CEO? After all, "high school dropout" isn't exactly the kind of credential you'd expect to see on a CEO's resume. It wasn't until my husband and I scaled our company to over a million dollars that I realized we needed someone to take charge of the CEO duties to keep everything from spiralling into disarray. So, I took the plunge, believing it was in the best interest of the company to assume the title. But after a couple of years in the role, the initial excitement quickly faded, leaving me with nothing more than an impressive-sounding title that felt empty and job duties I'd rather pull my hair out than perform.

In short, I was CE-Over it.

For a while, I felt like life was attempting to steer me in a new direction by hurling unexpected challenges my way, ultimately leading to my admission to the ICU. Stress has been said to manifest as illness within our bodies... and yet, even after my release and recovery, I chose to ignore all of the signs. The idea of quitting my business felt more daunting than continuing on, despite how misaligned and miserable I felt. So, I did what I knew best: I kept pushing forward. Quitting had never been an option for me, especially with a new store opening, a signed lease, and significant investments already made. I learnt what it felt like to be stuck between a rock and a hard place.

I'd been deeply engaged in self-development for a long time, focusing primarily on growth, hustle, and achievement. This mindset had undoubtedly helped me grow my business significantly. However, I've come to realize a substantial gap in the self-development community: advice on what to do when you've self-developed so much that you've outgrown certain aspects of your life. As we strive and evolve, it's inevitable that we will outgrow certain areas—so then what?

I can't count the number of books I've read urging me to "never quit" which made me feel like closing my business was not an option, despite how misaligned it felt. However, I soon discovered that quitting and letting go are crucial parts of the growth process. Clearing out unaligned aspects of our lives is essential for making space for better opportunities. I want to emphasize that quitting a job, career, relationship, or anything else that no longer fulfills you, is one of the bravest and most empowering actions you can take. One piece of advice I always give those contemplating significant changes is to avoid making life-altering decisions when emotions run high. Decisions made in frustration or anger can lead to regrettable choices. Instead, wait for your emotions to settle to ensure a clear, conscious decision.

After my hospital stay, I realized that I needed to prioritize my health and wellness, particularly addressing my weight, which had fluctuated throughout my life. At my heaviest, I weighed 270 lbs. I came to understand that obesity could lead to serious health issues if ignored, regardless of any "body positivity" mindset that I was being bombarded with. To transform my ingrained habits, I had to embrace three key elements: awareness, acceptance, and responsibility. For too long, I had made excuses and validated my size. Taking responsibility for my metabolic health was challenging, but it eventually became easier as I adopted healthier habits. I lost 70 lbs by focusing on whole foods, cutting sugar, quitting alcohol, and finding enjoyable ways to exercise. As I embraced this new healthy lifestyle, I felt increasingly inauthentic running a business that contradicted my new values. This led to cognitive dissonance—the unease we feel when our actions contradict our beliefs. We all encounter this in various ways: we eat foods that we know will make us feel bad, drink too much alcohol despite knowing it will make us sick, and buy unnecessary items even after promising ourselves we'd save money. It's the struggle between recognizing the negative consequences of our behaviours and giving in to strong short-term desires that overshadow our guilt. As a result, we overlook the repercussions and seek instant gratification instead. I encourage you to think about how cognitive dissonance shows up in your own life. What do you do that you know you probably shouldn't do? What do you do that makes you feel guilty? The first step in figuring out a solution to any problem is to simply recognize that there is a problem.

How could I continue operating a bakery business knowing how detrimental refined sugar and processed foods are to human health? How could I promote, sell and advertise products that I stopped polluting my own body with, to others? I couldn't. It all felt so wrong. It would be like a vegan owning a butcher shop or someone in sobriety owning a brewery. It started to drive me insane, and the guilt kept creeping in the more that time went on. Eventually, I decided that something had to give, and after everything that I'd learned regarding health, wellness and nutrition, there was no way for me to feel authentic or proud of running my bakery business if I continued. I couldn't unlearn this and I couldn't keep this business going.

Chad had worked full time in the business alongside me, and it was our main source of household income, so I knew I needed to share my feelings about it with him. It didn't take much convincing for him to agree. "I think it's pretty obvious that owning a cupcake shop was never my dream," he said with a smirk. I couldn't help but laugh.

As grateful as I was for his support in running this business, I realized I had overlooked the fact that he had been sacrificing his own dreams for mine. While that may sound honourable, it wasn't a destiny I would ever want for someone I was married to. Individually pursuing our life's purpose is how we create inner happiness and meaning in our lives. Sacrificing that for anyone else's dreams would be a shame. I was relieved that he wouldn't be upset about moving on to a different career, and it appeared that the relief was mutual. I quickly learned that encouraging those closest to us—spouses, friends, and family—to embrace their own authenticity and pursue their own dreams is the only way to express unconditional love.

And just like that, a cascade of events unfolded—from the tumultuous transition from artist to CEO, my terrifying stint in the ICU, embarking on a transformative health and wellness journey, followed by my husband finally looking forward to pursuing his own dreams. We decided to close the business and we bid a bittersweet farewell to Chick Boss Cake.

Now that I've shared my journey of how I ended up here, the rest of this book is dedicated to helping you discover your own authenticity. I will share my tips and tricks so that you can learn how to realign yourself as you continue to outgrow areas of your own life. Before you dive deeper into this book, I urge you to make a promise to yourself: commit to taking action on the strategies that resonate with you. As an author, it's disheartening to pour my heart and soul into writing this book, only for it to gather dust on a shelf. Your journey to authenticity deserves to be lived—not just read. Take charge and make every insight count. Make the most of your reading time by taking away at least three actionable points from this book to implement. Treat this as a rule for every book you read in the future. Yes, even if it's Fifty Shades of Grey—hell, there's probably way more than three takeaways if we're talking about Fifty Shades of Grey. Refuse to be someone who endlessly reads self-help books while making no real changes in your life. Don't trick yourself into thinking you're making progress when you're not taking action. Remember, learning life-changing information without applying it only deepens the disconnect between your beliefs and actions. Embrace the power of change and take decisive steps toward a better you!

Just because closing my bakery business was the right decision didn't make it any easier. Closing a chapter, regardless of the reasons, always brings undertones of sadness, grief, anxiety, and fear of the unknown. Announcing it to the public stirred a vast array of mixed emotions, as you can imagine. Our customers were sad, our staff and vendors were disappointed, our landlords were angry, and the haters and competition were thrilled. It was a mishmash of feelings that I wasn't entirely sure how to handle. All I knew was that I needed to accept the fact that everyone else's emotions and opinions were none of my business; the only person whose approval and acceptance I needed at this point was myself.

Would it have been easier to just keep running my business? Probably.

Would it have made other people happier? Of course.

Was it even an option? Absolutely not.

We overestimate the importance of adding to our lives while underestimating the transformative power of subtraction.

To create space for the extraordinary, you must be willing to let go of the ordinary. Embrace the strength to release what no longer serves you, because within these acts of courage lies the path to your true potential. You must be willing to let go of mediocrity in order to make room for the magnificent.

Chapter Two

INTERNAL INVENTORY CHECK—WHERE ARE YOU CURRENTLY AT?

Before delving into the details of assessing your current state and the alignment of your life, it's crucial to highlight two essential qualities that are vital for realignment and for living your most authentic life. I recommend pausing at this chapter for as long as necessary to fully understand and embrace these two skills. Without them, nothing in your life will feel aligned or authentic. Take the time to re-read this chapter and conduct any additional research to enhance your *self-awareness* and *vulnerability*.

In order to make genuine changes in our lives, we must learn to be brutally honest with ourselves and conduct what I like to call an "internal inventory check." This process can feel uncomfortable and even defeating at times, but it is imperative for our growth and development.

Vulnerability

- *Noun:* Willingness to show emotion or to allow one's weaknesses to be seen; the readiness to risk being emotionally hurt.

Self-Awareness

- *Noun:* Conscious knowledge of one's own character, feelings, motives, and desires.

Vulnerability and self-awareness are fundamental aspects of our human nature. As children, we are naturally attuned to our feelings, likes, and dislikes, expressing them openly and without fear of judgment. For instance, consider toddlers having meltdowns in public—they don't feel embarrassment. While their parents may be mortified, the toddlers are simply expressing their emotions in a raw and authentic manner. Although their self-awareness is still developing, it exists in a limited capacity, allowing them to connect with their feelings. So, what happens to our vulnerability and self-awareness as we grow up?

Society and social conditioning take over. Adults teach children that it is not socially acceptable to express vulnerability. They encourage kids to filter themselves so as not to offend or upset those around them. At a very young age, we learn to feel shame, guilt, and embarrassment regarding our vulnerability instead of being taught how to openly and kindly express our true feelings. As a society, we've worked hard to suppress our vulnerability, inadvertently teaching those around us that it's also unacceptable and unsafe for them to be vulnerable too.

Vulnerability: The Key to Authentic Connections

At the time of writing this book, I'm in my mid-thirties, and it wasn't until a few years ago, after watching Brené Brown's TED Talk on vulnerability, that I realized how crucial it is to our collective existence and how removed it has become from our culture. Before watching that talk, the mere thought of vulnerability made me feel nauseous. It was so uncomfortable that it took me several months after viewing Brené's talk to even begin practicing it. My stomach churned like a front-loading washing machine stuck on the heavy-duty cycle as I heard her voice in my head reiterating all the reasons why vulnerability was essential to our human experience.

Before that point, I was probably one of the least vulnerable people you would have met. However, thanks to Brené's transformative teachings, I started fully embracing and appreciating my own vulnerability. I know for sure that if I could remove the protective barriers I had strategically placed around myself to keep deep emotions and vulnerability at bay, then anyone else can do it too.

Growing up, I learned very early on that vulnerability was unacceptable and even detrimental to my well-being. My childhood was challenging; my father had significant anger issues, and if I didn't act in a way that he deemed acceptable, I would be punished. This environment taught me that I wasn't allowed to have feelings and, more importantly, that expressing them was intolerable. I remember one particular occasion when I confided in my mom about how my dad was hurting my feelings and making me feel upset. She innocently suggested that I write a letter to him expressing my emotions, which sounded like a logical and appropriate idea at the time. My mom has always had a peace-making mentality, so I took her advice. I poured my twelve-year-old heart into that letter, completely opening up about how I felt and hoping to help my dad understand how his behaviour was negatively impacting me, with the hopes that he would stop. However, to my embarrassment and devastation, my letter was met with laughter and sarcasm. My heart sank, and I felt anger toward my mom for suggesting the idea. I was even angrier at myself for believing that pouring my heart out would change his behaviour. In that moment, I learned that if it wasn't safe to open up and be vulnerable with my own dad, then it certainly wasn't safe to do so with anyone else either. Looking back now, I have a lot of empathy for my dad's own lack of emotional maturity back then. He was so uncomfortable with his feelings and vulnerability that he couldn't understand or accept mine.

After enduring the constant chaos and volatility at home, I eventually moved out and dropped out of high school at the age of 16. Navigating the adult world as a teenager thrust me into a perpetual state of fight-or-flight. Unknowingly, I was training my nervous system that a continuous state of stress, anxiety, and hypervigilance was normal. The fight-or-flight response is a powerful survival mechanism that all humans can activate when faced with immediate danger. Unfortunately, mine lacked an off switch, staying active for nearly two decades. I lived in a constant state of alertness—always on edge, skeptical, critical, and feeling unsafe, even in situations that most would consider perfectly harmless. Because this heightened state became my "normal," I didn't realize how abnormal—and deeply unhealthy—it truly was.

If you've experienced any kind of trauma, especially in your childhood or adolescence, I encourage you to evaluate whether you're still operating from a default state of high stress and anxiety. This may feel challenging to identify, as it likely feels normal—or even comforting—to be this way. However, it's crucial to identify this pattern so you can learn to re-regulate your body, mind, and soul. When we've trained ourselves to keep our guard up, stress becomes our normal state of being, making us unaware that it is completely abnormal and deeply unhealthy. I created many defenses to shield myself from vulnerability, a feeling I used to equate with "weakness." These included sarcasm, humour, bitterness, deflection, and defensiveness. The walls I built did exactly what I intended—they kept people at a safe distance.

This reminds me of an example from the movie *How the Grinch Stole Christmas* (the version with Jim Carrey). The film flashes back to the younger version of the Grinch before he became grinch-like. He decides to confess his feelings to a crush, only to be laughed at and ridiculed by the other kids for thinking a green, furry creature like him could ever be loved. Embarrassed and hurt by the negative reaction from his peers, he vows never to put himself in that position again and isolates himself from everyone. As a result, he lives a miserable, depressing life until he experiences kindness, empathy, and acceptance from little Cindy Lou-Who.

Negative situations in our early development can create deep wounds that, when left unaddressed, prevent us from experiencing true love and building strong, meaningful connections with others. The more we work on becoming comfortable with our weaknesses, emotions, and vulnerabilities—and the more we open up to people we feel safe with—the more normal vulnerability will begin to feel.

It's helpful to practice this with people who possess the emotional intelligence to engage in deep, meaningful conversations without judgment. Be aware that not everyone in your life may be in a healthy place to do this, and it's important to recognize those who aren't. Failing to do so could lead to embarrassment or humiliation, making you feel worse for trying. Finding a good counsellor or therapist with whom you connect is always a great alternative if you don't feel comfortable practicing vulnerability with those in your life. They have developed professional skills to listen and support people from a third-party, objective perspective.

Many people claim they've tried therapy and found it ineffective. Typically, it's not the therapy itself that doesn't work, but rather that they haven't connected with the right therapist. When looking for a therapist, it's a good idea to conduct a brief interview with them before beginning to ensure you feel like they're a good fit for you. Don't give up after your first attempt at therapy; not every therapist will feel right for every person. I've seen several therapists throughout my life, and it has been an integral part of my healing journey.

Take a moment to reflect on your earliest memories that made you feel embarrassed or ashamed of sharing your vulnerabilities and feelings. Do you still have walls up that prevent you from opening up today? Think of the people in your life. Is there anyone you feel truly comfortable being vulnerable around?

Even a simple shift in how we perceive vulnerability—from a weakness to a strength—can be a major step in the right direction. Whether with a friend or a professional, the more you practice embracing your own vulnerability, the more it will become your new normal. Soon, you won't be able to suppress it any longer. As you experience the joy of connecting more deeply with others and yourself, you'll begin to care less about anyone else's reactions to your newfound openness.

Over time, you'll find that even in the presence of people who lack emotional intelligence, their ignorance no longer fazes you. The benefits of living a vulnerable life far out-weigh any critiques from those who are stunted in their own growth journeys. I learned years ago to never take criticism from someone I wouldn't take advice from. I often remind myself of this. Being vulnerable is what makes us human. The more we embrace this, the more authentic and alive we'll feel. If you find yourself being vulnerable and someone responds negatively, remember how crucial vulnerability is to our existence. Meet their reaction with empathy and compassion for what they're lacking in their own lives. Here are a few things you can start doing right now to help develop your own vulnerability:

1. **Tear Down the Walls:** Start by noticing the moments when you put up emotional walls. Is it when you're feeling insecure? Or when you're trying to

hide your true feelings? Call yourself out—write it down, speak it out loud, or even tell a friend. Acknowledging the walls we've built up is the first step to letting them down.

2. **Have a "Heart-to-Heart Challenge":** Pick someone you trust and challenge yourself to have a real, unfiltered conversation. It doesn't have to be deep right away—just talk about something that makes you feel a little exposed. It could be a fear, a recent struggle, or something you're excited about. Make it a game: how honest and vulnerable can you be?

3. **Celebrate Your Flaws:** Take something you're insecure about—whether it's a quirky habit, a past mistake, or a perceived weakness—and turn it into your "badge of honour." Own it in a conversation with someone. For example, "Yep, I'm disorganized—but I'm working on it!" This simple shift in how you talk about yourself can inspire others to drop their guard, too.

4. **Take Bold Emotional Risks:** Do something bold that requires you to be emotionally exposed. Share an opinion you usually keep to yourself, admit when you don't know the answer, or ask for help when you normally wouldn't. The leap might feel risky, but each act of vulnerability builds your emotional courage.

5. **Keep A Journal:** Write in a journal or use the notepad on your phone to keep track of each time you've allowed yourself to be vulnerable. Whether

it's admitting a mistake, expressing a fear, or simply showing up as your true self—write it down. Watch the list grow as you embrace more moments of openness, reminding yourself that vulnerability is becoming part of your everyday life.

Cultivating vulnerability is a courageous journey with significant rewards. Embracing vulnerability unlocks deeper connections between ourselves and others. Each small act of openness strengthens our emotional resilience, empowering us to live fully. Remember, vulnerability is not a weakness; it's the key to true strength and genuine connection. As you take these steps, you'll feel more free, confident, and connected. With practice, it becomes easier and more natural. Soon you'll be stepping into a life filled with authentic connections, boundless joy, and the courage to be unapologetically yourself.

The Art of Self-Awareness

Let's shift gears now to talk about self-awareness. Developing a greater sense of self-awareness is a skill that we can continue to improve upon over time, just as we would develop vulnerability or any other skill. It starts by being honest with ourselves about the fact that we often avoid admitting our own shortcomings and negative behaviours because they're frequently perceived as weaknesses in our society and culture. However, the freedom found in developing our self-awareness far outweighs any short-term discomfort we may experience in the process.

To become self-aware means to develop a deeper understanding of our own thoughts, emotions, behaviours, and motives. It involves recognizing how our internal state influences our actions and interactions with others. Developing our self-awareness requires regular introspection and self-reflection. Here are five things you can do right now to help you gain a greater sense of self-awareness:

1. **Reflect on Your Behaviour**: Journal or take time to think about your actions and emotional responses. Ask yourself why you react a certain way and how your past influences your present. Understanding these motivations can lead to valuable insights and personal growth.

2. **Practice Mindfulness**: Spend a few minutes each day focusing on your thoughts and feelings without judgment. This helps you observe your mental patterns and increases your awareness of the present moment.

3. **Seek Feedback**: Ask friends or family whom you trust for their perspective on your behaviour and responses. Their insights can help you see blind spots and gain a better understanding of how you come across to others.

4. **Identify Triggers**: Pay attention to situations or interactions that provoke strong emotional reactions. Recognizing these triggers can help you understand underlying issues and improve your responses in the future.

5. **Limit Distractions**: Reduce time spent on social media, watching TV, or other distractions that pull

your attention away from your inner thoughts. Learn to get comfortable sitting in silence with yourself. This allows for deeper self-reflection and understanding.

One of the biggest advantages of enhancing our self-awareness is that we no longer need to hide parts of ourselves out of fear that others will notice or criticize us. When we are self-aware, we understand our strengths and weaknesses, so we won't feel offended by others' observations.

For example, let's say you're a perfectionist (like me). This means you can be very difficult to please, exceptionally nitpicky, painfully critical of anyone's work (especially your own), and far too detail-oriented for the average person to understand. If you've acknowledged and accepted all of this and worked on becoming self-aware, you'll already know this about yourself. Then, when someone points out that you're being too much of a nitpicky perfectionist, it no longer triggers an emotional response because you're already aware of it; they're just pointing out the obvious. Your weaknesses will begin to feel more like facts instead of personal attacks.

Can you see how much freedom and confidence you'll gain from working on your self-awareness? Suddenly, you're taking back your power and not allowing anyone else the opportunity to make you feel bad by attempting to trigger your flaws, pain points, or perceived weaknesses. As humans, we are meant to feel connected to each other, and the only way to do that is by developing our self-awareness and viewing our vulnerability as a strength. The more we show others our vulnerable side, the safer we make them feel to do the same. We cannot create true, meaningful, deep connections with partners, friends, family, or loved ones if we're not willing to be vulnerable and self-aware.

Developing self-awareness isn't always easy—it often means facing uncomfortable truths about ourselves that we would prefer to ignore. But this discomfort is key to growth. By reflecting, practicing mindfulness, seeking feedback, identifying triggers, and minimizing distractions, you'll become more in tune with who you truly are. The rewards are massive: stronger relationships, better emotional control, wiser decisions, increased resilience, and a deeper sense of personal growth. Start small, stay consistent, and watch the transformation unfold.

Initiating Your Internal Inventory Check

Let's begin the internal inventory process by examining which parts of our lives bring us joy and which need reevaluation. As humans, we naturally find happiness in growth. Personally, I thrive on development and feel fulfilled when engaging in activities that teach me something new—a skill, a perspective, a lifestyle—anything that improves my life. What surprised me most about this growth process was the realization that embracing new experiences required me to realign my life with the new knowledge I gained. I was completely unaware of this until I was deeply immersed in my health and wellness journey while running a million-dollar sugar empire. My new health-focused lifestyle felt completely unaligned with the past version of myself.

If we don't take time for an internal inventory check, we may fail to identify which aspects of our lives need realignment as we grow. Ignoring this leads to internal conflict, unhappiness, cognitive dissonance, and unfulfilment. I experienced this firsthand while managing my bakery and pursuing my health journey. I felt uneasy and inauthentic selling cake and sugar when I was trying to avoid them in my own life. It just felt wrong.

In my early twenties, I indulged in cake and sugar, unaware of their negative impacts. As my passion for a healthy lifestyle grew, I became fascinated by what I learned. Before closing my bakery, I would promote cake at work and then come home to watch documentaries about the dangers of sugar. Naturally, I began to feel disconnected from my business, but I couldn't pinpoint why until I asked myself a crucial question:

"Would the person I am today start this same business tomorrow?"

The answer was a resounding no. It wasn't a maybe; it was a firm and confident "hell no." So why was I still running a business that my current self wouldn't choose? I realized I was subconsciously prioritizing comfort over change. I had poured so much time, money, and energy into my bakery that I feared what the future held without it.

You can ask yourself this same question in various contexts to help clarify what needs realignment:

- Would the person I am today ______________ tomorrow?

- Would the person I am today start this same business tomorrow?

- Would the person I am today marry the same person tomorrow?

- Would the person I am today seek the same job or career tomorrow?

- Would the person I am today choose to be friends with this person tomorrow?

If you're like me, you might feel frustrated when you ask yourself why you're still doing something your current self wouldn't choose to do now. This frustration is an opportunity for growth. By recognizing the misalignments in your life, you can begin to make intentional changes that reflect who you are today. Embrace the discomfort of realignment; it's a necessary step toward living a more authentic and fulfilling life. Remember, change might be daunting, but the rewards of realigning your life to match your growth is the key to the fulfilment you've been seeking.

After realizing my business was unaligned with my values, I started asking those same questions about every other aspect of my life too—my friends, my husband, my hobbies, and more. Spoiler alert—my husband made the cut. You may find that some of these things have only remained in your life simply because they've always been there, even though they no longer align with who you are today. I hope you've identified people, places, and things that you've outgrown through this introspection.

We must be brave enough to let go of what once served us in order to create space for unimaginably better circumstances. This process will involve sitting in the emptiness for a while, which can feel like a deep, dark void before anything spectacular arrives. However, it's crucial to hold space for yourself and maintain your new standards. It's going to feel more challenging before it gets better, but trust that the Universe will realign you with everything that matches the person you've become—and it will be better than you ever imagined.

After reflecting on what no longer aligns with your values, let's dive deeper into how your current life feels to you. Here are another couple of questions to ask yourself:

- If you could describe how your life feels right now in one word, what would it be?

- Now, how do you *want* your life to feel? If you could sum that up in a single word, what would it be?

Often, when we're not living authentically or intentionally, these words end up being the polar opposites. For instance, you might describe your current life as chaotic while *wanting* it to feel peaceful. This disparity creates internal conflict, especially when we aren't living in alignment with our true aspirations. Don't feel bad if your words clash; simply acknowledge that you desire something different—something better. It takes immense courage to admit that our lives aren't as fulfilling as we wish, and even more to recognize that we may be the architects of our own dissatisfaction.

It's easy to point fingers at our bosses, careers, partners, or circumstances, but ultimately, we are responsible for our own happiness. Everything in our lives exists because we're actively choosing it—the good, the bad, and the ugly. The sooner we accept full responsibility for our role in our own suffering, the sooner we can begin the journey toward healing. If you continue to blame external factors for your unhappiness, you'll remain trapped in that cycle of suffering. Let this moment of clarity be the catalyst for change, guiding you toward a more authentic and fulfilling existence.

From Surviving to Thriving

Contrary to popular societal belief, our lives are not meant to feel stressful or hard. We are meant to face and overcome stressful and hard situations (this builds resiliency). However, when stress and hardships become ingrained in our daily lives, we need to recognize this as unalignment and something that needs to be reevaluated and changed. It's easy to believe that living in a chronic state of stress and hardship is normal when the majority of our population is living this way as if it's their only option. It is not their only option... and it is not your only option. In fact, it shouldn't even be an option! I need you to let go of this old belief so that we can work together on elevating our lives to unimaginable heights.

First, I want you to consider where in your life stress is most evident. What are the specific areas that consistently bring you stress? Identifying these sources is crucial because once we pinpoint the aspects of our lives that create ongoing stress, we can explore two key choices:

1. **Eliminate Stressors**: We can completely remove these stressors from our lives, making space for more aligned and authentic opportunities to emerge.

2. **Transform Our Response**: If we choose to keep these stressors, we must change how we respond to them. This involves setting healthy boundaries and reshaping our perception, so we no longer view them as "stressful."

Neither option is right or wrong, and there will be times when option one will feel most appropriate and times when option two will be. Both options above have pros and cons associated with them.

<u>Eliminating Stressors</u>: If your job is a constant source of stress—meaning most days feel stressful, hard, unenjoyable, or miserable—then eliminating this stressor by searching for a new career may be a sensible solution. This approach doesn't apply if you generally love your job but experience occasional stress. As mentioned previously, stressful situations are a normal part of life; it becomes problematic when stress is a regular occurrence rather than a situational issue.

Before you begin your job search, it's essential to pinpoint the exact sources of stress in your current position. If you don't do this, you might end up switching jobs without solving the problem, landing in a similar situation at a different company. This is where self-awareness plays a crucial role. I've seen many people apply to work at my bakery, stating that they left their previous jobs due to a stressful, fast-paced environment. Did they really think my bakery would be any different? With our higher volume, it's actually even busier, which could lead to more stress for them. This illustrates the risk of making a lateral move without recognizing what is truly causing the stress. We often fall into this pattern when we lack self-awareness. Instead of recognizing the real underlying issue, we blame outside factors—like the company—for our stress.

On the other hand, maybe you love your job duties and enjoy your work environment, but realize that your boss is the main cause of stress in your career. In which case, a lateral move could serve you well by finding a new company with a new boss but keeping similar job duties. It's all about getting to the root causes of why we feel the way we do. I'll insert a word of caution, though—if your main point of contention at work has to do with not getting along with your boss or coworkers, the more you learn how to communicate and work collaboratively with difficult people, the better off you'll be. Treat it as a challenge to overcome when working with people you'd prefer not to. As long as there's no abuse or blatant misconduct, it is actually a perfect opportunity to learn how to set boundaries and improve your communication skills.

Speaking of communication skills, many people believe they are effective communicators. However, it's important to understand that true communication is measured by how well others understand you. This means you need to adapt your communication style to fit the person you're talking to. The better you can connect with people from different backgrounds, ages, and cultures, the more effective you will be as a communicator. Remember, the best communicators aren't just those who speak well; they are the ones whose messages are understood and resonate with others.

Eliminating stressors doesn't just pertain to careers. We can choose to eliminate toxic relationships, bad habits and unhealthy environments in all aspects of our lives.

<u>Transform Our Response:</u> In this section, we'll explore how to keep identified stressors in our lives while learning to change our reactions and responses. Developing healthy boundaries is key.

A great example of this would be if you have kids. For some reason, it's frowned upon to utilize option one and eliminate them from your life altogether, even though they may very obviously be a major contributor to your daily stress. Crazy, right? Sometimes there may be certain phases they go through that can be incredibly stressful for you and can last lengthy, extended periods of time. Another example could be family, friends, or other people in your life who create significant stress but whom you do not want to let go of completely. It's essential to develop tools and strategies that allow you to maintain healthy boundaries and de-stress from these relationships. Self-care and therapy are effective strategies to help you manage stress. Establishing healthy boundaries means creating a reasonable distance between yourself and the stressors. Learn to pick your battles strategically when dealing with kids, family members, or anyone else in your life. Be intentional about when to engage and when to conserve your energy. If you're feeling tired, annoyed, or moody, it's safe to say that being around stressful people will not be a smart energy expenditure. Once you start to pay closer attention, you'll be surprised at how often our own responses and reactions to situations end up creating most of our undue stress.

Maybe you find that it's your partner or spouse who is creating a lot of stress in your life. First, I suggest addressing your concerns with them and trying to resolve the issues together or with a therapist if it's something worth salvaging for you. Otherwise, it may be wise to explore the option of letting them go and making space for a better connection. The closer we are to people in our lives, the harder it becomes to establish firmer boundaries, especially when we live with them and are supposed to be in partnership. Living with a partner whose behaviour causes constant stress can be extremely unhealthy and detrimental to our well-being, especially if they're unwilling to get help, change, or address our concerns constructively. If they truly love you, they will not want to intentionally inflict pain or hurt. Growing up in a tumultuous household, I knew that walking on eggshells, name-calling, and yelling would not be part of any romantic relationship I would engage in. I'd rather be single with cats—and I don't even like cats. I decided that if I were to marry or partner with someone, I needed to feel loved, safe, and appreciated, and I wasn't going to settle for anything less. These are my standards for relationships, and I firmly believe we teach others how to treat us based on the standards we set for ourselves. If you currently accept yelling, manipulation, or disrespect, then it's time to reevaluate your standards and raise the bar. No one deserves to live unhappily or in fear. It's true that disagreements are part of every relationship, but you can have respectful disagreements without name-calling or raising your voice even a decibel above your regular tone. If you're with a partner who loves you and cares about your feelings and well-being, they will respond with love. Romantic relationships should feel like a safe place; otherwise, what's the point? Wouldn't you rather live alone and in peace than with someone who makes every day miserable? I know that I would.

Improving any area of our lives begins with holding ourselves accountable and eliminating the victim mentality. In any stressful situation that we want to change, we must first identify and accept our role in contributing to the stress. If you've consistently allowed your spouse to treat you poorly, call you names, or be mean to you, it's crucial to recognize your role in enabling that behaviour. Doing so will help you develop self-respect, confidence, and higher standards for yourself. Otherwise, you run the risk of repeating the same unhealthy relationship patterns with every new partner you encounter. If you don't like how someone is treating you, it's your responsibility to set appropriate boundaries or remove them from your life entirely.

Whew. This chapter was intense, and I'm sure it sparked realizations that made you question various aspects of your life, or at least encouraged you to see them from new perspectives. It may have stirred both positive and negative

emotions, which is a great sign of self-awareness and vulnerability. For me, it was excruciatingly hard to admit that
I'd fallen out of love with the business I'd poured my heart
into for over a decade. Initially, I justified my thoughts,
telling myself that sugar was fine in moderation and that
many others run bakeries selling unhealthy treats—so why
should I feel guilty? But the very need to justify my feelings
was a major red flag.

I'll leave you with this: the authentic truth never requires
justification. Trust yourself enough to recognize what feels
right and what doesn't. Remember, every time you stand
firm in your truth, you empower yourself to break free
from the chains of self-doubt and societal expectations. So
never forget: your journey is uniquely yours, and the only
validation you need comes from within.

Chapter Three
THE SCIENCE OF HAPPINESS

Ah, happiness—the motivating driver behind everything we do, whether we're aware of it or not. It's the very thing that every single human is desperately seeking but often unable to sustain. If you ask anyone what the one thing they want out of life is, their response is likely to be happiness. Any other responses, such as success or freedom, are basically code words for happiness. From the moment we're born, we embark on what often feels like a never-ending quest for happiness. Yet, despite our best efforts, many discover that happiness can be elusive, often seeming just out of reach when we believe we've found it.

We're conditioned to believe that certain "things" and "achievements" will make us happy, and that if we work hard enough to obtain these, we will achieve happiness. The problem is that eventually, we end up obtaining these things and accomplishing those achievements, only to realize that we are no closer to happiness. We might celebrate and rejoice for a short period until we're on to the next goal or achievement that we hope will guarantee us happiness, and so on and so forth. This creates a never-ending loop that we get stuck in. Until we learn how to cultivate true happiness in our lives, we'll never experience the very thing we all say we want the most. The search for happiness can't be found anywhere; it's something that's created internally, not sought out externally.

It actually takes quite a bit of intention to create a life that feels happy most of the time. This is because we're wired to default to negative emotions, as we are pre-programmed with a negativity bias. Naturally, we experience a wide range of emotions, and this fluctuation is completely normal. However, it is entirely possible to retrain our brains to start defaulting to positive emotions instead. The amount of time it takes to reprogram your brain will depend on your current baseline of happiness, which results from a combination of mental, emotional, environmental, and lifestyle factors, sprinkled with a little bit of genetic predisposition. I was fascinated to learn that science tells us that 30-40% of our happiness levels are genetic, according to positivepsychology.com. This means that we inherit a certain level of happiness from our genes when we're born. While it may seem like a large portion of our happiness is determined by genetics and out of our control, let's focus on the positive and recognize that 60-70% of our happiness is something we can influence. When I think back on my own self-development journey, I realize that my natural baseline for happiness was quite low. I didn't feel like I had inherited many happiness genes. However, through my own efforts, I now see myself as an optimistic and happy person. We have the power to significantly improve our happiness levels, regardless of our genetics. In this chapter, I'll share various strategies to help you do just that. But first, let's address a common misconception about positive thinking and how to steer clear of something called *toxic positivity*.

The Toxic Positivity Trap

Toxic positivity occurs when someone dismisses or suppresses negative, sad, or hurt emotions, trying to replace them with positive ones—even when those negative feelings are completely normal responses to challenging situations. This mindset is harmful to our well-being and isn't something we should strive for. Negative emotions are a natural reaction to tragedies, trauma, difficulties, and unfortunate circumstances. Instead of trying to push these feelings away when they arise, acknowledge them, feel them, and create space for them. Be curious about why you're feeling this way and ask yourself what triggered those emotions. Was it something trivial, like spilling your coffee? If so, consider minimizing the time you spend upset over minor matters so they don't ruin your day. Or was it something more significant, like the loss of a loved one? How long your negative feelings linger depends on the situation and your resilience. Don't rush through these emotions; instead, take the time to analyze them so you can support yourself appropriately. Seek out helpful resources that can guide you through specific traumatic experiences, such as therapy, counselling, talking with a friend, or practicing self-care.

One approach I've found particularly beneficial when dealing with traumatic events and emotions is to seek out books, podcasts, and videos on topics that resonate with my experiences. While it may seem like a small step, hearing the perspectives and suggestions from people who have gone through similar situations can be incredibly helpful. We can't always expect those in our immediate circle to understand what we're experiencing, but thanks to the internet's accessibility, we can often find others who have shared similar experiences. There's a unique connection that occurs when we hear advice from someone who has walked a similar path, and it can be deeply healing.

I discovered the power of this connection a couple of years ago when my beloved dog, Bianca, passed away. As someone who has chosen not to have children, my pets are my babies, and this apricot-coloured miniature poodle was my absolute bestie. She brought immense joy to some of the most challenging years of my life. I got her as a puppy when I was just eighteen, a few years after I moved out of my parents' house at sixteen. She remained the only constant in my life during a time where nothing felt stable, and chaos ran rampant. I was shuffling around from apartments, to friends' couches, to motels, to park benches, to moving in with a boyfriend, to moving back out, to moving in with a new boyfriend, to ultimately becoming so depressed that I thought about killing myself to relieve me of this erratic volatility. My adolescent years were undoubtedly traumatic. The one reliable source of joy in my life at the time was that little fourteen-pound, curly-haired, brown-eyed, floof of happiness. Beyond just comfort, she often gave me a reason to live. I loved her with all of my heart and though my brain logically knew she wouldn't live forever, my soul fully expected her to. I knew no matter how long she lived, it would've never felt long enough. When she died at the age of sixteen, to no surprise, I was devastated. The pain of losing a pet is completely underestimated in our society and unless you've been there and can relate, I wouldn't expect you to understand.

When it comes to grief and loss of life, if it's someone or something of significant importance in your life, then it's going to hurt, regardless of whether it's an animal or a human. The meaning and connection you have with them is what determines the severity of pain, not the species. Since not everyone in my life at the time was able to relate to the grief that comes from the loss of a pet, I felt very alone and isolated in my feelings. I felt guilty for being so devastated when I knew people who had seemingly bigger losses, such as deceased parents, spouses, and children. Why should I be so upset about a dog who reached their documented life expectancy? I was trying to override my very raw emotions with logic, which, by the way, never works.

I knew my family and friends were sympathetic and well-intended, but I didn't feel like anyone truly understood what I was going through, nor did I expect them to. To be honest, I didn't even understand what I was going through myself. It wasn't until a friend recommended a book to me. It was called *The Grief Recovery Handbook for Pet Loss* by John W. James and Russell Friedman. *I remember thinking to myself, What the fuck is a book going to do to help me grieve my dead dog?* Turns out... a lot. It was the most helpful resource that I could've laid my tear-drenched hands on.

In hindsight, I can now see why it was so instrumental in my grief recovery, and it was because of the relatability factor and the validation of my feelings. Knowing that I wasn't alone in feeling the way that I did made me much more open and receptive to the advice and tips laid out in the book. Though it didn't take all of my pain away, it did provide me with concrete tools to help mitigate the pain, and it allowed me to move forward with my life while treasuring Bianca's memory.

If you're struggling with any form of grief, I strongly encourage you to seek out people who have gone through similar losses and connect with them. I will also mention that the same authors of the pet loss recovery book have another version that's not tailored to pets but more so loss in general—death, divorce, health, and other significant losses that we experience in our lives—and it's called *The Grief Recovery Handbook*. I highly recommend it.

Not only do we want to avoid falling into bouts of toxic positivity ourselves, but we also want to be cognizant of not projecting our toxic positivity onto others during their most vulnerable times either. I say this because, in our culture, we do this all too often without even thinking about it. As soon as someone confides in us about something they're struggling with, we automatically go into damage control, repair, and recovery mode. I am absolutely guilty of this myself, and if you grew up in our Western culture, then you probably are too. Not only are we conditioned to hate being vulnerable, but we are even more uncomfortable when others are vulnerable in our presence. It becomes so unbearable that we cannot stand it, so we end up blubbering away, conjuring up any ounce of positivity we can possibly think of to remedy the situation. Though our intentions are generally well-meaning, this often leads to the vulnerable person feeling more isolated. They may feel bad because they are unable to absorb or implement our misguided positivity in their deepest moments of sorrow. This can result in them feeling even worse than they did in the first place. People going through hard times don't give a fuck about our positive spins on their shitty situation. The best thing we can do is to be quiet and hold space for them. We should validate their feelings and hug them if it feels appropriate. We can also ask how we can help and offer to do simple things to make their life slightly easier. This could include making them tea, coffee, or dinner, helping around the house, or running errands, etc. Oftentimes, just sitting in discomfort when someone else is hurt or suffering and sharing your healing energy with them is more than enough. No one who's hurting expects you to take their pain away. When you try to, it can come across as though you're dismissing their feelings. This may lead them to feel worse because you're telling them all the ways they should feel happier when they just don't. Don't project your toxic positivity onto others in their most vulnerable moments.

Another important point about toxic positivity is that people tend to distrust those who always seem perfectly put together and happy. This facade is unrealistic and unrelatable. Even as someone who embraces positivity, I find it incredibly inauthentic and frustrating when someone constantly covers up their own negative feelings just to maintain a positive outlook. Even worse is when they launch into an unsolicited TED Talk about how I should minimize my own feelings. Instead, let's focus on normalizing real emotions and having authentic conversations. Silver linings are great, but they shouldn't replace our genuine feelings. In my experience, most situations (aside from tragedies and deaths) do have some silver lining, but we're often unable to recognize it while we're in the midst of the emotional struggle. We need time. The silver lining usually only becomes apparent well after the pain and negative feelings have been appropriately resolved and we're back to feeling like our normal selves again. For instance, say someone is going through a really terrible divorce, and it takes them a year to deal with their emotions. It's excruciating at first—extremely painful, unbearable at times. They have to learn how to do everything on their own again, and it feels lonely and scary. Then one day, after the pain subsides and they're in a healthier place, they end up meeting their actual soulmate (like for real, for real this time, someone who makes them seriously question their taste in previous partners). They realize that this is true love. Life is so much better than it ever was with their previous partner. That terrible divorce that they went through can be attributed to the silver lining of meeting their new partner. Pain is a necessary part of the healing process, and sometimes we just have to take out the trash to make room for the treasures.

In summary, the trap of toxic positivity can stifle our emotional growth and fracture our connections with others. When we dismiss or rush through our negative emotions, we deny ourselves the richness of human experience. Instead of pushing away discomfort or forcing a constant sunny outlook, let's lean into the authenticity of our feelings and create a safe space for others to do the same. It's in the messy, vulnerable moments that true connection flourishes. Remember, healing is a journey that unfolds in its own time, allowing us to unveil the silver linings that often lie hidden beneath the surface of our pain. So let's celebrate the ups and downs, knowing that it's all part of what makes us beautifully human. Now, let's get back to the science of happiness.

Yikes—this chapter on happiness took a sharp detour down a dark path talking about death and divorce. In actuality, I'm happy that this chapter took a turn because the reality is, if I kept this chapter bright and fluffy as one might have predicted, it wouldn't have encapsulated the true reality of happiness. That is, without deep sorrow, we cannot experience heightened levels of happiness. This is the law of polarity at work, where everything in the world has equal opposites. No one is humanly capable of being happy one hundred percent of the time (and we just talked about why we aren't going to try to be, thanks to toxic positivity). What we want to do is aim for the majority, overall vibe and feeling of our lives to be happy.

Think of it like this—as though all of your experiences in life were divided into positive happy ones and negative unhappy ones, and they were placed onto a judicial scale. All the negative ones on the left side and all the happy ones on the right. Though there will be weight on both sides, we want the scale to tip as far to the right as possible, resulting in an overarching theme of happiness in our lives as a whole. There's no question that there'll be some heavy weight on the left side for all of us to bear, but with intention and resiliency, we can influence the scale to tip happily in our favour.

Through a blend of research and personal experiences, I'm thrilled to share with you the true science of happiness. I've organized this knowledge into distinct sections, complete with insights for each, allowing you to identify where you can grow and where you're already thriving. Our ultimate goal? To elevate every key area outlined below, empowering you to cultivate a profound sense of joy and tip the scales of happiness intentionally in your favour. Here are the seven keys to unlocking the science of happiness:

<u>Health and Wellbeing</u>

Though these are not in any particular order, I will say that this is the first section because it *is* the most important. The rest of the sections are important but essentially pretty meaningless unless you have your health and wellness in order. In case you haven't heard this saying, I'm going to leave it right here for you to ponder: A *healthy person has a million dreams, whereas a sick person only has one.* Reflect back on any time you've ever been sick. Did you care about anything other than simply getting better? Without our health, it becomes incredibly hard to focus on anything else, including our happiness. It's not just about being physically fit, but about having the energy, mental clarity, and emotional stability that comes with it, all of which are the foundations to a happy life.

Health and wellness have always been a challenge for me, and for most of my life, I struggled with weight issues, stress eating, lack of motivation, and poor dietary choices. It wasn't until the past few years that I made the serious decision to take control of my health. Before that, my habits were a catastrophe—I was drinking litres of wine regularly, binging on candy and chocolate after dinner like it was an Olympic sport, relying on takeout, and guzzling caffeine as if it were my lifeline. Late-night cravings were a regular thing—usually for McDonald's McFlurries, which I enjoyed despite my lactose sensitivity (because who needs a digestive system, right?). Meanwhile, my idea of exercise was limited to the highly intense sport of rapid hand-to-mouth movements. My sugar addiction was so intense that, at one point, I wouldn't be surprised if refined sugar made up over half my daily caloric intake. Owning a bakery during that time only fuelled my unhealthy relationship with food. But through it all, I've learned that the more I invest in my health, the more happiness I can cultivate—when I feel better physically, my mind is clearer, and I have the energy to go after what truly fulfills me.

The result of this death prescription I was obliviously prescribing myself was morbid obesity (270 lbs), severe brain fog, depression, anxiety, fatigue, joint pain, inflammation, among a myriad of other things likely brewing below the surface that I wasn't aware of. These conditions didn't just affect my physical health—they drained my energy, impacted my mood, and left me feeling stuck in a negative cycle that killed any chance of happiness. When I tell you that I was a mess, I mean... I was a fucking mess. I just didn't know it because it all seemed normal and socially acceptable at the time.

I started developing healthy habits very slowly—one tiny micro habit at a time. I introduced each new habit one by one until it became a natural part of my routine, and I didn't have to think about it anymore. Once a habit was ingrained, I would add another, gradually building on my healthy habits. This process is known as habit stacking, a strategy I learned from the book *Atomic Habits* by James Clear. Each small, healthy change didn't just improve my physical state—it gave me more energy, lifted my mood, and boosted my confidence. Happiness followed naturally. It's crucial to take your time with this process. If you try to change too much all at once, you'll likely get overwhelmed, give up, and fall back into your old habits. I went through that cycle multiple times before I finally figured out how to adopt a healthier lifestyle.

First, I decided to quit gluten, which greatly reduced my brain fog and improved my fatigue. After that, I took on the keto diet, which meant cutting out sugar entirely. Let me tell you, this was no easy feat, especially since I owned a bakery stocked with sugar from floor to ceiling—it was fucking hard. However, I managed to get through it by using stevia-sweetened alternatives to help me cope with the sugar withdrawals. Giving up sugar was a significant step for both my physical and mental health. Sugar is infamous for causing mood swings, inflammation, energy crashes, cravings, and anxiety. Eliminating it really helped me regain control over my mood and energy levels.

After that, I decided to give up alcohol entirely (another bitch of a thing to quit). Again, alcohol is a known depressant, and removing it from my life gave me clearer thinking, better sleep, and—most importantly—more emotional resilience, which plays a huge role in maintaining our happiness. Quitting alcohol also opened my eyes to society's heavy reliance on external crutches to cope with a life many of us are dissatisfied with, forcing me to confront the uncomfortable truth that real joy must come from within.

Finally, and most recently, I cut down on caffeine after learning about the negative impacts on women's hormone health. Thank goodness for decaf, otherwise, I would've really been in for a wake-up-and-smell-the-coffee moment if I had to give up my favourite beverage in the whole entire world.

Most notably, I recently closed down my million-dollar bakery empire because of my growing cognitive dissonance toward processed foods and sugar. As I've mentioned throughout my book, my bakery business no longer aligned with the health-conscious woman I have become. I see the closure as a powerful symbol marking the end of my old, unhealthy self and the beginning of my renewed commitment to a healthier, more authentic version of myself. This decision wasn't just a career change; it represented a profound shift towards living in alignment with my values, which has brought me a deep sense of peace and happiness.

Even if your health and wellness seem okay right now, there's always room for improvement. Nothing pays higher dividends than adding new healthy habits and letting go of old, unhealthy ones. Your body is the foundation of your happiness—when you treat it well, everything else in life becomes easier. Unfortunately, due to the high consumption of processed foods, many people find themselves trudging through their days with low energy, lack of motivation, and complete exhaustion. This drain on vitality hinders their ability to engage fully with life, ultimately diminishing their capacity for joy and fulfilment. This energy deficit is directly linked to their diets, elevated stress levels, and a lack of purpose, and it should never be considered normal. If you believe any of these symptoms are acceptable, I urge you to raise your standards.

The foods we eat can significantly impact our moods and emotions, either positively or negatively. Numerous studies highlight this connection, with emerging research showing an even closer link between gut health and brain health. However, you don't need scientific studies to recognize this; just think about how you feel the day after drinking too much alcohol or an hour after indulging in fast food. What's your mood like then? It's clear that what we put into our bodies influences our emotional wellbeing, longevity, and overall health. To feel good mentally and emotionally, we must fuel our bodies with foods that support our wellbeing.

One key lesson I learned early in my health journey is that if you're not actively and intentionally pursuing health and wellness, you're inadvertently heading toward illness. There is no middle ground that is safe or okay. You're either moving towards one or the other. Doing nothing means you're allowing yourself to slip into poor health, and poor health will always rob you of your happiness. I'm not going to get into all the ways to improve your health. There are countless books, podcasts, and resources dedicated to enhancing your health and well-being, created by experts far more knowledgeable in this area than I am. A couple of my favourite authors in this field are Dr. Casey Means and Dr. Sara Gottfried. My hope is that I've inspired you to care about the number one contributor to happiness and to feel fed up enough to do something about it!

<u>Growth and Learning</u>

Growth and learning are the catalysts for true happiness—every step forward and lesson learned fuels our sense of purpose as we evolve into the best version of ourselves. It doesn't matter if you're learning through the traditional school system or pursuing personal self-development; the key is to keep learning continuously. Personally, I'm a strong advocate for self-development because it helped me discover a way to actually enjoy learning. In contrast, the traditional school system often felt frustrating to me—like having to ask for permission to use the bathroom in high school and being forced to partake in subjects like algebra, which made me want to pry my eyeballs out with a spoon.

That said, while self-development can be a rewarding journey, it's important to recognize that the self-help and self-development industry is still an industry. It is not devoid of outlandish marketing schemes, false promises, cheesy advertising tactics, or money-hungry "gurus." I've seen many people in this space overstep the boundaries of genuine help by offering astronomically priced workshops, conferences, and "exclusive retreats." I actually fell victim to one myself. It was a weekend workshop that promised to scale small businesses and thoroughly educate entrepreneurs on all aspects of business to ensure proper growth and success strategies. It was called 10X360, and while I won't draw further attention to the scumbags who run this workshop, it ended up being a complete scam with a $40,000 price tag. The information taught throughout the weekend was laughable. For a course that's supposed to cover all "three hundred and sixty degrees" of a business, it left out, in my opinion, one of the most important components—customer service. That's right; there was no discussion of customer service, retention, or satisfaction at any point. The workshop was shoddy and juvenile at best—a clear reflection of the scam artists running the program. It taught me an expensive lesson—not everyone in the self-development industry has your best interests at heart. We must apply the same level of discernment in navigating this space as we do in other aspects of life. There are countless workshops, courses, conferences, and coaching programs that promise to improve your life and provide success, freedom, and happiness, often with exorbitant price tags. If it seems too good to be true, or if someone is charging an outrageous fee to teach you something, they're looking to make bank—not a difference.

If you decide to spend your money on these programs, make sure you trust the person running them, or use disposable income and be prepared to take a gamble. There are many other workshops and conferences that I've happily paid for because I admired the person running them and felt they had good intentions, and I ended up gaining a lot from those experiences. Just remember to think critically and be cautious—that's all I'm saying. We all crave the keys to freedom, success, and happiness, and it's all too easy to get lured in by people and programs that claim to hold the secrets to achieving them. By selecting your resources wisely, you can turn this adventure into one filled with fulfilment and joy, rather than disappointment. Seek out those who truly inspire you—those whose teachings align with your values and whose success stories are backed by real results.

In conclusion, growth and learning are vital for a happy life. Research shows that lifelong learning boosts mental health and overall well-being, with studies linking continuous education and skill development to greater life satisfaction and lower anxiety and depression. Learning releases happiness hormones that foster long-lasting joy and motivation, encouraging us to pursue new experiences rather than just seeking fleeting spikes of instant gratification. Personal growth fosters resilience, enabling us to cope better with stress and setbacks—key components of happiness. As we learn and grow, we often also end up connecting with like-minded individuals, creating a sense of community that further enhances our happiness. Thus, actively pursuing growth and learning is essential for cultivating a richer, more joyful life.

Relationships

Friends, family, and our intimate partner (if we have one) are a crucial piece of the happiness equation. Creating deep connections with people in our lives is the most beautiful gift. Just think about how insignificant you would feel if you lived your entire life completely isolated on your own and then died, and that was it. No one to share special moments, meals, or experiences with. That couldn't sound more miserable if it tried.

In one of Arthur C. Brooks' books, I read about how when we do something alone, it's okay, but when we add people we care about to share the experience with, it makes it memorable and heightens our level of happiness remarkably. Studies show that people with strong social connections are 50% more likely to report happiness than those with fewer connections. I did not recognize the significance of this until I started to pay attention to it in my own life. I would mindlessly hang out with friends or attend the odd family gathering with no awareness of the fact that these indeed were life's most cherished moments. Now that I've drawn this connection thanks to Mr. Brooks, I remind myself of this often and melt into the presence of those I care about most. I often take a moment during my time spent with others to think about how happy and grateful I am to share that moment with them. Do you ever think about how much of a gift it is to be in the presence of others? People are sharing their most valuable asset with us—time. We typically don't draw this conclusion until after we lose them, but I assure you it is much more beautiful and rewarding to appreciate them while they're still alive. We are strange creatures when you think about how under appreciative we can be when we're in the physical presence of our loved ones and how devastated we end up being when we lose them. Still, for some reason, we have a hard time truly grasping the significance of their presence. The next time you find yourself surrounded by loved ones, imagine this—an hourglass suspended above each person's head, partially filled with sand as it spills out distressingly fast towards the bottom of the glass. The sand represents the amount of time they have left in their physical bodies on earth. How differently would you treat the time you spent in their presence? What else would you say to them before you parted ways for the very last time? Surely, you wouldn't be in a rush to leave if you saw that their hourglass was on its final grains of sand, knowing this would be the last time you got to be with them forever.

This got me thinking: why do people save all the good things to be said for funerals? How meticulously thought out and heartfelt are the eulogies we give after the person is no longer here to hear us say all the things we wish we would've said to their faces? We're eager to pour our hearts out as we grieve, yet we often end real-life encounters with nothing more than a casual "talk soon" or "love you." I have to share with you the definition of *eulogy*: "A speech or piece of writing that praises someone or something highly, typically someone who has just died." How much deeper, closer, and more meaningful could it be if we delivered eulogies to our living loved ones? Why don't we praise them highly while they're still alive so that they can truly feel and experience the depths of our love for them? Imagine how transformative it could be to express our admiration and gratitude openly, creating an atmosphere of love that nourishes our relationships.

Again, our lack of vulnerability as a society makes this feel awkward or difficult, but it's fundamentally easy to do if you open your heart and embrace your own vulnerability, as we discussed in Chapter Two. Take a moment to reflect on the closest people in your life right now and think about what you would say about them if you were speaking at their funeral. Write it down and give them the letter or call them up and tell them. Don't let another day pass without expressing your feelings. Praise your loved ones highly while you still have the opportunity to do so. Deep, meaningful connections are what makes life worth living and thus greatly impact our happiness levels.

Remember, happiness isn't just a destination; it's a byproduct of the love and connections we cultivate along the way. When we invest time and energy into our relationships, we create a support system that can weather life's storms, bringing us joy even in challenging times. Cherishing these bonds is not just beneficial for our loved ones but is a profound gift to ourselves, reinforcing our sense of belonging and purpose. Ultimately, the quality of our relationships can shape our happiness in ways that nothing else can.

Career

Our modern society has done a pretty good job at perpetuating the idea that work should be hard and there's no need for it to feel rewarding, impactful, or, dare I even say... fun? I mean, it makes sense. How else would modern society convince people to work forty hours a week in a factory on an assembly line, doing the same redundant tasks over and over every day? Factory jobs pay well for a reason—few people actually dream of becoming a production line worker. It is one of those jobs that's a means to an end—admittedly, a respectable one for the person who is just trying to provide a living for their family. But was it their dream? Are they excited to wake up in the morning to go to work? Or do they just accept their fate, clocking in and out day after day, each moment bringing them one step closer to their retirement fantasy?

If you're thriving in other areas of your life and don't *mind* your job—like, you don't love it, but you don't hate it either—and feel comfortable with where you're at in your career, then by all means, keep doing you. If all the other areas of happiness are flowing abundantly well, then maybe you can get away with this area providing a little bit less happiness and fulfilment while continuing to tip the overall happiness scale in your favour. However, if you're yearning for something more, remember, you didn't pick up this book to settle for mediocrity. You're destined for greatness, and it's time to unleash your full potential. I encourage you to consider that forty hours a week adds up to a significant amount over the course of your lifetime. Think about the sheer amount of life we spend at work in our careers. For me, it's not an option to trade my time for money at a job that does not light me up. Period. I can't even think of a worse value vs. trade proposition.

I understand the need to do what you have to do in the short-term to provide for yourself and your family—ab-solutely. However, don't allow yourself to be held hostage by a job solely for the pay, benefits, sick days, free products, vacation days, or any other superficial justification. There are countless career options that can fulfil your financial needs while also providing meaning and purpose to your life. The ideal career for anyone is one where you get to serve others by doing work that utilizes your unique gift or skill set. This connection to service not only enhances personal satisfaction, but also fosters a sense of belonging. We each have so much to offer the world, and just think about how much smoother, more efficient, and happier society would be if more people assumed roles that made them feel energetic, aligned, fulfilled, purpose-driven, and enriched. When individuals find joy and meaning in their work, it creates a ripple effect, improving overall societal well-being.

I know there are many things to consider when pursuing a career, and pay and benefits are certainly among the contending factors. But when did we decide that it has to be either/or? Why can't we have the career of our dreams *and* all of those extra benefits? Consider asking yourself these questions:

What does success look like to me?

Is my current role aligned with that vision?

It's disheartening that the last thing we typically consider is whether the job is something we're actually excited to do or if it will allow us to utilize our gift in a fulfilling way. It's alarming that external factors like pay, benefits, and vacation days often take precedence over our happiness at work. Achieving harmony between our professional and personal lives is essential for overall happiness. It's crucial to ensure we have time for personal interests and relationships outside of work, as this is vital for maintaining our mental health and satisfaction.

We also need to continuously reevaluate whether the job we've held for the past ten years still aligns with the person we are today. Surely, you've grown and evolved over the last decade into someone different from who you were at the beginning of your career. Is your current career still in sync with who you've become? This is exactly what I recently had to consider and reassess in my own journey. I started my bakery business brimming with passion and excitement for creating sugar-laden treats that were both creative and irresistible. The twenty-two-year-old me had a blast at the beginning of my bakery career. However, as my passion began to shift toward taking care of myself, losing weight, eating whole foods, and becoming healthier, I realized I was now a completely different version of myself. It's never an easy realization when we become aware of the inevitable. I understood what I needed to do. I could have chosen to ignore my inner voice, drawn in by the comfort of a well-paying job, but deep down, I knew I would be sacrificing my true happiness in the process. It is detrimental to our mental, physical, emotional, and spiritual health to stay somewhere that we know we no longer belong. It'll eat us alive from the inside out.

In a world that often prioritizes hard work over fulfilment, it's crucial to recognize that our careers should bring us joy and purpose, not merely serve as a means to an end. Sadly, many people settle for jobs that provide financial stability but leave them feeling unfulfilled. True happiness lies in pursuing paths that resonate with our passions and unique skills. As we reflect on our professional lives, we must ask ourselves whether our current roles align with who we are today and whether they contribute to our overall well-being. By embracing this pursuit, we not only honour our personal journeys but also elevate the collective happiness of our communities. So, take a moment to evaluate your career path—what steps can you take today to align your work with your passions and create a life that truly fulfills you?

Financial

The good old, "Money doesn't buy happiness," statement. Well, I'll tell you something... neither does poverty. I get the concept behind the statement about money not buying happiness, which is why I advocate for people to rein in their unintentional spending habits. However, it's important to recognize that a certain level of financial stability and freedom *does* contribute to happiness. Notice I said contribute; it is not the entirety of the equation. Happiness is the sum of all seven of these categories in this chapter combined. Since we are living in a society where money is required to gain access to basic needs such as housing, food, and healthcare—along with the things we don't need (but want) like vacations, gadgets, and entertainment—we can't deny that money can certainly influence our happiness levels.

The amount of happiness you equate to money really depends on your personal relationship with it. If you're someone who constantly needs to upgrade and buy all the latest stuff, seeking out "bigger, better, and more," to fill a void, then no... no amount of money will buy happiness. In contrast, if you use money generously and intentionally to improve your family's and community's lives, then yes... it quite literally can buy happiness. Equally important is the means by which you generate this money. Are you grinding, hustling, and working your life away at a job you hate in order to make more money? If so, please refer back to the previous section and consider a career change. Any money earned through grinding will never feel close to happiness—regardless of how much you make.

On the other hand, if you're making your money by doing what you love every day, the impact on your happiness will be profound. Someone who works at a job they hate may earn the same income as someone who works at a job they love, yet their feelings towards money and overall happiness will be completely different.

I've come across articles that attempt to pinpoint exact dollar amounts needed to achieve happiness, but I believe this approach is misguided. First, factors like inflation and varying economic conditions in different regions can significantly impact these figures. Secondly, since happiness is an emotion and a feeling, our overall happiness is more influenced by our individual relationship with money and our feelings about how we generate and spend it. To elevate our happiness through financial means, we must have enough money to cover our basic needs with a reasonable amount left over to enjoy life. Additionally, we must enjoy the work we do to generate that money and be intentional in spending it on things that are meaningful to us instead of on items that provide cheap dopamine hits and external validation. More on this in Chapter Four.

In conclusion, while money may not be the sole determinant of happiness, it undeniably plays a significant role in shaping our overall well-being. By striving for financial stability and using our resources wisely, we can enhance the quality of our lives and create more fulfilling experiences. Remember, it's not just about how much you earn, but how you earn and spend it that truly matters. So take a moment to reflect on your relationship with money—are you using it to enrich your life and the lives of those around you? Make intentional choices that align with your values, and let your finances support your journey to happiness. You have the power to transform your financial landscape into a source of joy and fulfilment.

Comfortability and Unpredictability

We need both comfort and unpredictability in our lives in order to gain a stronger sense of happiness. Comfort refers to our need for stability and security, while unpredictability encompasses the spontaneity and excitement that keeps life engaging. The amount of each will vary from person to person. It's important to learn how to recognize when we need to intervene to create more of one and less of the other. For the most part, we're wired to default towards comfort, making it challenging to seek out uncertainty (unless you're an Aquarius like myself, which might give you more of an appetite for adventure and change). Understanding our individual traits can help us assess how much comfort or unpredictability we naturally gravitate toward.

We often cling to comfort to avoid facing the reality of our own mortality. The fact that we will eventually die is hard to confront, so we seek safety in familiar routines and predictable situations. By holding on to comfort, we distract ourselves from the uncomfortable truth that life is temporary. This need for stability can lead us to overlook the beauty of stepping outside our comfort zones. It can keep us from experiencing the exciting and unpredictable moments that foster growth and happiness. Instead of embracing life's challenges, we may find ourselves stuck in a pattern of avoiding unpredictability. In doing so, we miss out on fully experiencing life and all of its richness.

The more flexibility we practice in navigating between comfort and unpredictability, the more resilience we develop. Research in positive psychology suggests that a balanced life, which includes both comfort and unpredictability, leads to higher levels of overall well-being and life satisfaction. Finding the right balance fosters personal growth, enhances creativity, and ultimately leads to a more fulfilling life.

In conclusion, embracing both comfort and unpredictability is essential for cultivating a fulfilling life. By recognizing the areas where you may be clinging too tightly to comfort or venturing too far into chaos, you can take intentional steps toward achieving a healthier balance. Challenge yourself to step outside your comfort zone and welcome the unexpected, as these experiences can lead to profound growth and joy.

Are you too comfortable and missing out on growth opportunities? Challenge yourself to step outside your comfort zone this week. Try something new, whether it's taking a different route to work, signing up for a spontaneous class, or engaging in an activity that excites you.

Or are you living too chaotically without any sense of stability? Reflect on your current routines and identify one area where you can introduce more comfort and stability into your life. This could be creating a cozy reading nook, setting aside time for self-care, cultivating healthier routines or establishing a calming evening ritual.

Healing and Forgiveness

I haven't heard too many people talk about the significance of healing and forgiveness in relation to cultivating lasting happiness, despite its undeniable importance of breaking free from emotional burdens. The burdens of resentment, trauma, and grudges are heavy enough to drown you in your own suffering, making it impossible to experience genuine happiness. Regardless of any negative or horrendous past experiences that have happened to us, we must be relentless in our pursuit of healing and forgiveness. In case you're not familiar with the author Louise Hay's work, she goes into great detail about how trauma and unresolved emotional pain manifests as real physical pain, disease, and illnesses within our bodies. I believe this to be true, and if you're still carrying around some heavy baggage from the past, I strongly encourage you to get her books and delve into her work. It's truly fascinating.

I used to hate hearing the phrase, "Forgiveness is for you, not for them." It didn't make much sense to me until I actually went through the process of forgiving people who had wronged me. Now, I completely understand. Forgiveness isn't just about saying the words "I forgive you." It's a conscious decision to release the grip that past pain has on your life. It requires intentional effort, and it doesn't happen overnight. It's not something you can simply declare and be done with. Forgiveness is an ongoing practice that takes time and commitment. You have to keep working at it, feeling a little lighter each time, until one day you realize you no longer need to practice it—because it has finally happened.

You'll know you're nearing true forgiveness when you can think about the person or situation that hurt you without feeling negative emotions. Full forgiveness is reached when you can think of them with genuine empathy and even wish them well. Forgiveness does not translate to tolerability. You're under no obligation to offer second chances, and it's entirely possible to forgive someone without their knowledge or involvement. Apologies are a "nice to have," not a "must-have." I've learned to forgive people who will never know I've forgiven them, because it's for my own well-being, not theirs. Apologies only become necessary if you choose to invite that person back into your life. Personally, I refuse to welcome anyone back into my life without their acknowledgment of wrongdoing and a plan to prevent similar behaviour from happening again in the future. The chances of being hurt again by someone who hasn't accepted responsibility are far too high.

We all carry the weight of someone or something that we still need to forgive. Today, I urge you to take that vital first step toward healing—you'll be grateful you did. One powerful method that has helped me heal from every trauma, grudge, and injustice I've faced is writing a letter to express all my feelings toward the person or situation that caused me pain. Then, I burn that letter, watching as the ashes are swept away by the wind, releasing the burden and reclaiming my peace. And when I say write a letter… I mean, write a motherfucking letter! Leave nothing left unsaid and hold nothing back. It could be one page long or twenty pages long—just write until your heart has nothing left to say. When I first heard of this idea, I thought it sounded like it would never work in a million years. It seemed like a total waste of time and emotional energy. Yet, as ridiculous as it appeared, I couldn't believe how effectively it transformed my life. I was shocked by how quickly I was able to fully forgive, heal, and recover through this practice. After burning those letters, I felt an incredible weight lift off my shoulders, leaving me with a profound sense of peace. I hope you'll give it a try. This method is grounded in therapeutic practices that emphasize the power of expression to release pent-up emotions, creating greater mental clarity and emotional freedom. I believe it's so effective because the brain's subconscious doesn't distinguish between sharing those feelings with the actual person and releasing them by putting them on paper. To the brain, all that matters is that you've finally cleared the heavy baggage from your subconscious.

The same letter-burning process also helps if you're grieving the loss of a loved one and have things left to say that you wish you had said. I've burned a few letters in my day, and all I can say is that I'm glad that the ashes are all that remains. This has allowed me the ability to rekindle some relationships and invite certain people back into my life (with the help of their own apologies and acknowledgments, of course). For others, it's allowed me the ability to peacefully wish them well on this journey we call life without them being part of mine. It's not about the reconnection, though; it's about the personal freedom and the long-term happiness you'll finally get to experience now that you've healed and forgiven.

Healing and forgiveness are powerful, transformative journeys that can reshape our lives. Though they may seem daunting, embracing these processes is essential for breaking free from the chains of resentment and emotional pain. Each step you take towards forgiveness is a step closer to reclaiming your happiness and lightness. Remember, forgiveness is not a one-time event; it's a continual practice that leads to profound personal freedom. I encourage you to start today—write that letter, burn it, and watch your burdens turn to ashes. As you release your burdens, you'll create space for joy, peace, and new beginnings. So take that leap of faith—prioritize your healing and commit to this journey of self-discovery. You deserve the happiness that awaits you on the other side.

Chapter Four

BENEATH THE SURFACE—VICES AND NEGATIVE COPING HABITS

This chapter isn't about perfection; it's about awareness. It's not meant to make you feel bad, guilty, ashamed, or inadequate. Instead, it aims to help you recognize negative habits that aren't serving you and to learn how to cultivate a healthier relationship with them—or, ideally, eliminate them altogether. I'll be sharing my personal struggles with my own vices to help you feel less alone in facing yours.

In order to reduce or eliminate our unhealthy vices and coping mechanisms, we must first be honest about the negative impacts they have on us. We need to stop justifying, rationalizing, and glorifying these behaviours. Over time, as you become aware of the triggers that entice you to indulge in your chosen vices and the consequences of these fleeting pleasures, you'll start to crave them less and less—perhaps even removing them from your life entirely.

Alcohol, drugs, smoking, shopping, gambling, processed foods (fast food, junk food, packaged foods, sugary desserts), and any product or stimulant that alters your mood or perceived state of happiness and well-being can be considered a vice. Notice that I said *perceived* state of happiness and well-being. That's because, though it may appear to temporarily improve your state of happiness in the short term, it actually harms your state of happiness and well-being in the long term. Until we can learn to live our lives contently without vices and the need to depend on them as coping mechanisms, we will never be able to experience true happiness. The first step in eliminating vices from our lives is to recognize that they are exactly that—vices. We have to stop labelling them as "fun" or "a way to relax, unwind, or de-stress." Instead of turning to some external vice, we should be asking ourselves what it is that's causing us to not feel like our life is fun, relaxed, or peaceful in the first place.

Recognizing these vices is crucial, especially because they often mask the underlying chronic stress we experience. Chronic stress is not conducive to living a happy and ful-filled life. It eats away at our mental and physical well-being, leaving us feeling drained and unfulfilled. That's why it's imperative that we identify the areas of our lives that have been contributing to our chronic stress. By doing so, we can address the root of our problems instead of relying on external vices for comfort. Ignoring these root causes only perpetuates a cycle of temporary relief and long-term suffering. Stress should only show up in our lives as random events, not as consistent states of being. Of course, our individual perceptions of stressors vary based on our own beliefs and past experiences, but I really want to reiterate the fact that stress should be a rare event in your life and not a common occurrence.

There have been many studies done on the detrimental effects of chronic stress, showing how it manifests into illness and disease within the body. This isn't just about feeling overwhelmed; it's about the very real health consequences that can arise from allowing stress to dominate our lives. Contrary to societal norms and cultural beliefs, it is absolutely possible to live a peaceful, low-stress life filled with happiness and meaning without using vices to cope. In fact, embracing healthier coping mechanisms will undoubtedly unlock a deeper sense of joy and fulfilment. Society doesn't want us to believe this because our economy relies heavily on our consumption of vices. In fact, the lower our collective baseline of happiness is, the more we end up turning toward vices, resulting in a more profitable, vice-driven economy. This leads to a harmful cycle, where we become accustomed to finding comfort in things that ultimately cause us harm. In other words, the happier, healthier, and more fulfilled we are, the less we'd need to turn to vices. This would result in less profit for big pharma, processed food conglomerates, the healthcare system, and all the rest of the vice industries (alcohol, tobacco, retail, gambling, etc.). This awareness should empower us to take control of our happiness and well-being, breaking free from societal constraints. It makes sense that their motives would be to keep us unhappy, unhealthy, and unfulfilled. After all, we are just dollars and cents to them.

You're not wrong in feeling like vices make your life *seem* better, happier, or more exciting. That's exactly what they're formulated to do—to make you believe that you need them in order to experience positive feelings and emotions in your life. The vice companies spend millions upon millions of dollars formulating their products to be highly addictive. Then, through their marketing and advertising, they convey the message that we need these things in order to live happily. It's just not true, and until you can fully surrender your vices without resentment or desire for them, you'll never experience true happiness. Vices are a massive industry, and while their marketing might lead us to believe that they will make us happier or improve our lives in some way, the reality is that they exist for profit—not for you, not for your best interest, but for profit. These companies will go to great lengths to manipulate and condition us, drawing us in repeatedly. It's time that we reclaim our power, make smarter, more intentional choices, and stop letting them exploit our vulnerabilities. Their sole agenda is clear: to keep us hooked at all costs.

Are you feeling triggered, annoyed, or defensive while reading this chapter? That's a strong sign that you know, deep down, that it's time to confront your vices. Our triggers are not just annoyances; they are profound teachers, guiding us toward the healing we desperately need. Each time you feel triggered by someone or something, seize the opportunity to unpack those feelings and address the underlying root cause of the pain. Our triggers serve as mirrors, reflecting the pain or discomfort within us that demands attention, love, and healing. By embracing and healing these triggers instead of resisting or avoiding them, we reclaim our autonomy and power. The more we identify and unpack our personal triggers, the less impact they will have on us in the future. This journey requires deep self-awareness, honesty, and accountability. Our society has become extremely over-sensitive and encourages us to avoid things that have the potential to trigger us, as well as to be overly cautious in an attempt to not trigger others. I couldn't disagree more. It is impossible to completely avoid triggering others, considering that everything we do or say could potentially be triggering to someone else. This cancel-culture mentality is weakening our resilience. I detest this feeble, whiny, cancel-culture attitude that has surfaced in our society lately. Your triggers are your responsibility; my triggers are my responsibility; their triggers are their responsibility. End of story. Tiptoeing around sensitive topics in attempts to avoid hurting someone's feelings is unhealthy and stunts our growth as individuals and as a collective society. Not to mention, when we feel the need to censor ourselves, we sacrifice our own authenticity in the process. The best advice I can give you is to be yourself and stop worrying about triggering others; let them work through their own issues. Their triggers have nothing to do with you, and they're none of your business. The same goes for you. If you find yourself triggered by someone else's actions, don't waste your time letting them know they've triggered you. I can pretty much guarantee they weren't intentionally trying to, nor do they care. View the trigger as a gift and an opportunity to unpack it, dedicating your energy and time towards healing it instead of sulking and acting out. If it feels appropriate, remove the triggering person from your life, but don't do so without first addressing your own trigger. Otherwise, it's only a matter of time before someone else triggers you again in the future. What we often overlook when it comes to triggers is that we actually need to experience being triggered in order to heal ourselves and build resilience. One way you might find yourself triggered by this chapter is through an overwhelming urge to immediately defend or justify your personal vices and coping mechanisms. Take a moment to reflect: which vices are you feeling particularly defensive about? Is it alcohol, smoking, shopping, gambling, or perhaps frequently indulging in processed foods like fast food, junk food, or sugary desserts? Acknowledge if any of the following justifications arise:

"I only drink on the weekends."

"I only drink red wine, which is healthy because of the antioxidants."

"Shopping makes me excited and happy, and I never go over my budget."

"I have money to spend, so may as well spend it."

"Fast food is how I treat myself after a long day."

"Smoking or drinking helps me to relax and unwind."

"Gambling makes me feel exhilarated, and it's how I have fun."

No matter what excuses you conjure up to justify indulging in your vices, it's essential to recognize that these are mere rationalizations. The good news? I'm not here to tell you to give up shopping or drinking altogether. As mentioned at the beginning of this chapter, we aren't aiming for perfection. Yes, it is proven that the fewer vices we indulge in, the happier we will be, but it's also important to give ourselves grace as we navigate cutting back on them. Cutting out as many vices from your life as you can will benefit you greatly. If you're unwilling to cut certain ones out completely, consider minimizing how often you indulge in them and ask yourself what emotional needs they're attempting to fulfil. This self-reflection can help you make more conscious choices that enhance your well-being rather than serve as distractions. What you choose to indulge in is entirely up to you. The quality of your life and the standards you set are yours to define; I have my own. However, the unwavering truth of this chapter is that you must take a stand and redefine your relationship with your vices, refusing to let them be your escape to numb the pain, unwind from reality, or seek fleeting moments of cheap pleasure.

Now, I invite you to join me on a journey of self-discovery as I share my own struggles with the vices that once held me captive: alcohol, shopping, sugar, and processed foods. Together, we'll explore how confronting these cheap dopamine hits can lead to profound growth. Join me at the end of this chapter for a dopamine detox to reclaim your power, reset your mind, and awaken a vibrant version of yourself that thrives on genuine fulfilment instead of fleeting highs.

Alcohol

Alcohol had been a prevalent part of my life for as long as I can remember—long before I even hit the legal drinking age, if we're being real. It never spiralled into a full-blown addiction; instead, it became my go-to escape for managing stress and numbing my emotions. In a world where alcohol flowed freely at parties, celebrations, and casual hangouts, it became an integral part of my social scene, becoming a prerequisite for connection and fun. Many individuals, myself included, often believe that if they don't have a blatant alcohol addiction, there's no reason to quit. This belief is dangerously deceptive, blinding us to the underlying reasons for our alcohol use. Many of us turn to it to escape uncomfortable emotions and situations, fostering unhealthy habits that stifle personal growth and overlook the myriad of detrimental health risks that result from alcohol consumption. As an introvert, I used alcohol as an anxiety anesthetic in every social situation. I didn't realize that it wasn't the alcohol I needed; instead, I had to learn to be more intentional about choosing aligned and authentic environments that didn't trigger my urge to escape. I also recognized the importance of limiting my time in social settings to allow myself space to quietly recharge in solitude. Introverts need their alone time like plants need sunlight.

Fast forward to today, and it has been two and a half years since I quit drinking alcohol. I won't pretend it was easy; it was one of the hardest vices for me to overcome. I used to love wine—white, red, rosé, sparkling; I loved them all. Visiting wineries was one of my favourite pastimes, especially since I lived close enough to Niagara's wine country to make a day trip whenever the mood struck. I never imagined that I could live a life without indulging in wine; the thought of it felt utterly miserable, boring, and devoid of fun. So many activities that I cherished revolved around enjoying a glass or two (or three or four) of wine—watching *The Bachelor*, networking events, girls' wine and cheese nights, weddings, birthdays, and any gathering, really. You can imagine the challenge I faced when I decided to eliminate the common thread that was woven throughout all those joyful moments—wine. Suddenly, I was acutely aware of its absence, which had been intertwined with so many of my cherished experiences. What was the point of life when wine and cheese night turned into just cheese night? It seemed un-brie-leavable!

As if that wasn't enough, everywhere I turned, I was being bombarded by an endless stream of marketing and advertising that insisted life without alcohol was a party no one wanted to attend. It was a constant reminder of what I was missing out on, amplifying the struggle to maintain my decision. It wasn't until I started my health and wellness journey that I truly began to notice how my body reacted to alcohol. The cognitive impairment it caused should've been a clear warning sign that it wasn't doing my body any favours. But beyond that, I often woke up in the middle of the night extremely dehydrated, and my mood would plummet for several days afterward. My body felt puffy and sore from inflammation, and I experienced prolonged fatigue and depression after a night of drinking. It was pure insanity how often I inflicted this suffering upon myself, knowing the consequences. Consider how often you've drunk, woke up with a hangover, and vowed never to do it again—I'd lost track of how many times I made that same promise to myself.

Through this journey, one truth became crystal clear: you'll never feel better, be healthier, or have more energy after drinking than if you didn't drink in the first place. Isn't it the definition of insanity to keep repeating this behaviour while fully aware of how negatively it will affect you? After starting my health and wellness journey, I couldn't help but wonder what kind of internal damage drinking was causing. This concern grew stronger in light of the clearly destructive external symptoms I was experiencing. Negative external symptoms often signal much deeper damage to our internal organs and bodily functions.

As I delved deeper into my research, I began to tune out the marketing and social acceptability surrounding alcohol. I discovered that alcohol is classified as one of the highest-level carcinogens, which means there is substantial evidence linking it to an increased risk of cancer in humans. According to the World Health Organization, "Alcohol is a toxic, psychoactive, and dependence-producing substance and has been classified as a Group 1 carcinogen by the International Agency for Research on Cancer decades ago. This is the highest risk group, which also includes things like: asbestos, arsenic, radiation, and tobacco."

Yikes. When was the last time you considered sprinkling a little asbestos on your food? The fact that this information is readily available, yet we still choose to buy into the marketing propaganda surrounding alcohol, is, at best, ignorant and, at worst, deadly and downright foolish.

Reflecting on the past, I couldn't help but draw parallels between alcohol's acceptance today and the way tobacco was once endorsed as a "healthy habit" by doctors in the 1950s. The medical community's approval misled many into believing that smoking was safe. It's just as absurd as if you went to your doctor today and they told you that having a few glasses of your favourite alcoholic beverages each week is perfectly fine. Such advice is ludicrous, especially in light of the growing evidence linking alcohol consumption to serious health risks. No one who is truly concerned for your health should ever suggest that consuming alcohol is safe. If you choose to drink, do so with the awareness that it is not healthy or safe and is recognized as a leading cancer-causing carcinogen. What's appealing about a cold, tall glass of a cancer cocktail, anyway?

Now, I know you might be thinking there's no way that you could ever quit drinking. Trust me, I understand how difficult it is to make that commitment (though I assure you it gets easier, and there are plenty of alcohol-free wines, beers, and cocktails on the market now). If you're not ready to commit to quitting yet, at the very least, be honest with yourself and acknowledge that it's not good for you. Stop justifying. Stop rationalizing. Start being honest. One of the most valuable lessons in self-awareness is recognizing bad habits for what they are, without any rationalization. Yes, red wine has antioxidants, but guess what? So do blueberries, dark chocolate, and pecans—without the cancer-causing components.

I'll admit, while learning about these negative effects of alcohol, I still drank it. But instead of pretending like it was perfectly fine and harmless to "have a few drinks a week," I began to acknowledge that I was consuming a toxic substance offering no real benefits—only a fleeting high that ultimately led to feeling terrible later on. This mindset shift alone prompted me to reconsider how often I touched a glass of wine to my lips; I realized that the momentary pleasure wasn't worth the inevitable hangover and guilt that followed. Ultimately, this mindfulness guided me toward cutting back substantially before quitting altogether. After all, when is it ever a good idea to willingly enjoy a flight, pint, or tall one of arsenic? I mean, alcohol.

I encourage you to be relentless in your pursuit of knowledge. We live in a world where lack of knowledge is simply the result of intentional ignorance. You have every resource at your fingertips, and anything you choose not to learn is your own failure to take responsibility. Recently, my local health unit launched an ad campaign that boldly stated, "Alcohol causes cancer. Now you know." I felt it was important to share that message in my book so that you know, too.

After about a year of slowly cutting back on alcohol to become a healthier version of myself, I started to feel an increasingly stronger sense of cognitive dissonance every time I took a drink. I was beginning to know better and felt guilty for not doing better. After my experience in the hospital, it became even more crucial for me to take control of my health. This meant not knowingly consuming a cancer-causing carcinogen in any quantity. So, I quit. My desire for health simply outweighed my desire to drink. Living an alcohol-free life feels like the fog that once clouded my mind has lifted, revealing clarity and joy I never knew was possible. I now indulge in a delightful array of non-alcoholic beverages—sparkling water infused with fruits, creative mocktails, and non-alcoholic wines—allowing me to enjoy healthier versions of my favourite beverages without the negative consequences of alcohol.

I no longer miss the ritual of pouring a glass of wine or the social pressure to drink. I embrace the new alcohol-free version of myself and get to create beautiful memories that, get this, I actually have the privilege of remembering. One thing that I didn't realize when I quit drinking was just how curious people would become about my reasons for quitting. Refusing alcoholic beverages at events continuously sparked the question: "Why don't you drink?"

First of all, this speaks to how heavily conditioned we are as a culture regarding the normalization of alcohol, to the point that it's shocking to people if you don't drink. Secondly, I use this as an opportunity to educate and spread awareness of the consequences of drinking, but only if I'm asked. I don't go out of my way to provoke these conversations with those holding a drink in their hand; no adult enjoys a lecture on their life choices. I am especially conscious of not passing judgment on those who drink because I was once a drinker myself and am empathetic toward all the factors that make it difficult to stop. Most importantly, I don't judge my friends who choose to drink around me. Being self-righteous never inspires anyone to make positive changes; instead, I choose to lead by example—showing that a fulfilling life without alcohol is not only possible but truly rewarding.

I cherish the clarity, connection, and vitality that come from living an alcohol-free life. Each day feels more vibrant, filled with authentic experiences and deeper relationships. I've discovered a renewed sense of purpose, better health, and a mind unclouded by the fog of drinking. I invite you to reflect on your relationship with alcohol and consider the incredible possibilities that await you in an alcohol-free life. Imagine waking up energized and ready to embrace each moment without regret. Take the bold step to re-define your idea of fun—join me on this journey toward greater joy, authenticity, and connection. Start by setting small, achievable goals for yourself, whether that's taking a break from alcohol for a month or exploring new social activities that don't revolve around drinking. Your most fulfilling life is waiting for you; all you have to do is say yes to it.

Sugar and Processed Foods

Another major vice that I struggled with was sugar and processed foods. Unlike alcohol, this was something I had battled with my entire life since childhood. I have this vivid memory that stands out from when I was a very young child—probably around three years old—when my first memory of a sweet treat was a banana popsicle. It was a hot, sunny day, and I was sitting on the curb with my mom, waiting for the local city bus. I still remember the way the waxy paper wrapper felt as my lips brushed against it, while fireworks propelled from my taste buds as I took my first lick. I'm certain that my love affair with sugar began right then and there. Still, to this day, nothing evokes nostalgia better for me than a banana popsicle.

As a child, I learned to use unhealthy foods as rewards, treats, and ways to numb feelings and cope with stress. Growing up in the nineties, when sugary cereals and ul-tra-processed foods ran rampant with seemingly no ill ef-fects or warnings, I developed extremely unhealthy eating habits at a very early age and never questioned them. The only question I'd ever asked myself when it came to food was, "What did I *feel* like eating today?" Have you ever made food choices based on the answer to this question? It's a slippery slope, isn't it? The food choices that follow that question are usually not optimal for health and wellness. Most people, myself included, wouldn't say that they felt like eating a salad.

This was a lifelong habit that was built and reinforced throughout decades of my life. These ultra-processed foods also happened to be more convenient and tasted better than their healthier alternatives, so it ended up being a no-brainer for me. My awful eating habits were normal to me, and I never saw anything wrong with them, regardless of the excess weight I ended up lugging around. I'd been obese since childhood, thinning out as a teenager, only to slowly revert back to obesity in my mid-twenties. It was no wonder that I started a bakery business. I'd always had a major sweet tooth and loved baking as a kid (which, in hindsight, was less about the baking and more about the eating of the baked goods), and as a result, I ended up morbidly obese for the majority of my life. Ultimately, this pattern of indulgence and weight gain became a painful reminder of my struggles, as I grappled with the impact of my choices on my health and happiness.

Reflecting back, I can honestly say that I didn't see anything wrong with my eating habits; I lacked the awareness to connect them directly to my obesity. My weight became a relentless battle between emotional eating and my futile attempts to shed pounds. I fell victim to every pill, supplement, and powder that promised miraculous results, only to find myself disappointed each time. Eventually, I reached my heaviest weight of 270 lbs in my early thirties, after nearly a decade of running my bakery business. Looking back, I can't say I'm surprised. I was trapped in my own game of Candy Land, surrounded by an endless supply of sugary treats, with each bite blurring the line between pleasure and pain.

Luckily for me, during this time, the body positivity movement was on the rise, and everywhere I turned, I was being told to love myself regardless of my size... and for a while, it worked. I accepted myself for being morbidly obese and stopped any proactive measures towards alleviating the issue. In my mind, I was simply embracing my body, but in reality, I was ignoring my health. In fact, I no longer felt that my obesity was an issue at all. Body positivity had given me permission to ignore the disease-ridden trajectory I was bulldozing towards. In hindsight, this was the worst movement and biggest trap I'd ever fallen for. The origins of this movement probably trace back to a corporate processed food company aiming to keep people sick, unhealthy, and addicted to whatever they were selling. I wouldn't be surprised. These industries are notorious for funding all kinds of studies to support whatever their biased best interest is, regardless of the truth.

I have a huge problem with the body positivity movement. Not because we shouldn't love our bodies—I'll explain when body positivity truly makes sense later—but because, as a morbidly obese woman, it was doing me no justice. It taught me that living in a state of disease (which is exactly what obesity is, according to the Centers for Disease Control and Prevention) was perfectly acceptable and something to be celebrated rather than a serious health concern. What kind of world are we living in where we feel the need to glorify a self-inflicted disease as being any sort of positive thing? If you're currently obese and having a hard time hearing this, just know that I, too, have been there. I know it's hard to hear. For a long time, I took refuge in my own ignorance, believing that body positivity justified my situation. It was difficult for me to accept when my doctor looked me straight in the eyes and candidly explained where my obesity would lead me if I didn't take serious measures to intervene. That moment shattered my complacency and marked the beginning of my journey from blind acceptance to painful awareness. That moment was a wake-up call that forced me to confront the harsh reality I had been covering up with a misguided notion of body positivity.

The truth is that the truth hurts sometimes. I was 270 lbs and morbidly obese. Not just a little fluffy. Not a little thick around the edges. Not big-boned. My body was made up of more than 50% fat. I was fat. I'm not saying this out of a place of fat-shaming or non-acceptance; quite the opposite. I'm saying this from a place of love and compassion because I care deeply about the health and wellbeing of myself and society as a collective. I've seen how drastically different life can be on the healthier side. Anyone who reassures you that you look fine or that your obesity isn't really a big deal is saving face and doesn't actually have your best interests in mind. I'd be leery of having someone like that in my life if I were you. They're too afraid to tell you the truth because of how it would make them feel to do so.

I understand how defeating and frustrating it feels to be overweight, especially when you lack the knowledge or energy to make necessary changes. It's a gut-wrenching sense of desperation and helplessness unlike anything I've ever experienced. This isn't about beauty standards or fitting into a specific size or number on the scale. It's about three crucial factors:

1. Your overall health

2. The length of your life

3. The quality of that life

People are living longer but ending up spending the last twenty years of their lives sick and debilitated in nursing homes, unable to take care of themselves. Is that what you want for yourself? I love when people use the excuse of "You only live once, so may as well enjoy it," or "I could die tomorrow, so may as well indulge today." I used to think this way too. Sure, you only live once... but you also only die once, too. What's your point? Wouldn't you rather feel vibrant, full of life, and with loads of energy every day? Does the *quality* of your life not matter to you at all? I'd rather feel my best every day and die knowing that I lived a high-quality life than stuff my face with misery. This isn't the time or place to justify your bad habits with statements like, "What if I died tomorrow?" Reserve that question for provoking positive changes, not for preserving unhealthy behaviours. Instead, ask yourself, "What if you actually lived tomorrow?" Why continue behaviours that damage your body and ensure you'll feel worse if you do live? Wouldn't it be worse to maintain unhealthy eating and drinking habits, knowing that with every passing day, you're getting closer to developing diabetes, cancer, or other diseases? If we don't feel discomfort about something, we'll never feel the need to change it. Personally, I'm surprised obesity isn't considered an eating disorder. Why is under-eating labelled as disordered eating, while overeating isn't, when both lead to illness and are forms of disordered eating? I'll be the first to admit that my unhealthy, overindulgent eating habits felt extremely disordered, especially compared to how I eat now. Disordered barely begins to describe the differences between my diet then and now.

According to the National Institutes of Health, "Obesity is recognized as a significant public health hazard, as it increases the risks for multiple diseases, such as type II diabetes, cardiovascular disease, hyperlipidemia, hypertension, stroke, breast and colon cancer, and degenerative arthritis. The cost of treating obesity-related conditions is estimated to range from 147 to 210 billion dollars per year. It decreases quality of life, functional capacity, and increases morbidity and mortality. Treatment has been shown to reduce morbidity and mortality. Therefore, preventing or treating obesity would be very beneficial on both an individual and societal basis."

What about this statement sounds remotely appealing? It's not just about those numbers; it's about the quality of our lives—your life, your family's life, and the lives of those in your community. It's time to change your health in order to change your life.

I understand that certain medical conditions, medications, and other health factors can play a role in negatively impacting our metabolic health. However, let's not allow external factors to be an excuse for letting ourselves deteriorate. There are many people living with the odds stacked against them who prioritize their health and, as a result, experience greater energy, resilience, and quality of life. With determination and the right strategies, it's possible to make choices that support our well-being, even in challenging circumstances.

As I mentioned earlier, I want to address what I believe the correct use of body positivity should be reserved for. I suggest using "body positivity" for things that are not within our control, such as scars, freckles, height, blemishes, discolouration, pigmentation, stretch marks, cellulite, abnormalities, wrinkles, aging, disabilities, or anything along these lines. Body positivity should not be used as an excuse for being unhealthy and obese. Additionally, it's not anyone else's place to point out, make fun of, or bully someone for being overweight or obese. First of all, it's none of your business to judge anyone else when we all struggle and are imperfect in some way. Second of all, how do you know they're not just starting out on their health journey? I started mine at 270 lbs, so there was a period of time when I was on my health journey, but sure as hell didn't look like it. We all have to start somewhere. There are many obese people who are taking necessary steps towards a healthier life, and therefore, making anyone feel bad about themselves for any reason is unacceptable and makes you a weak individual. I guarantee that you have enough of your own shit to work on in life, so stop worrying about the people around you. You have your own journey to focus on.

In order to transform into a healthier version of yourself, you must begin living as that person today, regardless of your current appearance or circumstances. This means adopting the new habits and routines that align with a healthier lifestyle, even if you still look and feel overweight or unhealthy. It might be uncomfortable at first, and you may face resistance from both yourself and others, but it's essential to take those initial steps. Imagine how a healthier you would approach daily choices—prioritizing nutritious meals, staying active, and nurturing your mental well-being. You can't expect to become something different without changing your daily habits; transformation starts with the actions you take right now. Embrace this journey with the understanding that every positive choice you make lays the groundwork for the vibrant, healthy life you envision for yourself.

To truly overcome unhealthy eating habits as a result of using food as a vice, you must first get to the root cause of your relationship with food. Are you using it as a way to cope with stress, filling an emotional void that needs to be addressed? Perhaps like me, you find yourself binge eating in moments of anxiety or sadness, seeking comfort in food when life feels overwhelming. Acknowledging whether you have a food addiction is crucial; it's not just about the physical act of eating but also about understanding what drives you to seek out food as a solution. By exploring these personal issues, you can begin to peel back the layers and identify the mental or emotional struggles that are often intertwined with unhealthy eating patterns. This process of self-reflection is vital, as addressing the underlying issues is essential for creating lasting change. Only by confronting these root causes can you begin to heal and develop a healthier, more balanced relationship with food.

A final word regarding sugar and processed foods—they are destroying our health. Sugar leads to obesity and weight gain, and it's a major player in the rise of type two diabetes. Processed foods are full of unhealthy fats, added sugars, artificial ingredients, and seed oils, all of which fuel inflammation and increase the risk of chronic diseases like heart disease and cancer. Eating a diet packed with refined carbs, sugar, and processed junk wreaks havoc on your metabolism, damages your gut, and leads to issues like insulin resistance and digestive problems. And it doesn't stop there. Sugar creates cravings, making it hard to break the cycle and stick to healthier habits. The more you eat it, the more you want it—keeping you stuck in a cycle of poor health and low energy. The bottom line is that if you're serious about improving your health, you've got to cut back on sugar and processed foods. Not next week. Not tomorrow. Now. Your body—and your future—depend on it.

Shopping

Mindless shopping was another vice I had to overcome, and much like alcohol and sugar, it was extremely difficult due to the fact that it was a habit I'd begun forming at a young age. I don't know about you, but when I was a teenager, the thing to do was hang out at the mall. Most of my allowance money I'd earned was spent at Ardene's, and anything left over was put to use at Bulk Barn in the candy aisle (surprise, surprise).

Oftentimes, we end up developing these habits early on and fail to reevaluate them or question them at any point. It's obvious when we purchase something and experience that quick dopamine hit to our brain that we begin to equate shopping and buying material things to happiness. It quite literally triggers a happy chemical response. Combine this with all the marketing and advertising being shoved down our throats to keep us coming back for more—talk about a choking hazard.

After much reflection and accountability, I realized that most of my shopping habits came from a place of boredom. I would be especially vulnerable when I was scrolling through social media, falling prey to all the ads that were desperately vying for my attention. Social media has a way of creepily knowing everything you didn't know that you surely don't need. Of course, when the ads pop up to make us aware of it, all of a sudden, we feel like we most definitely cannot live without it. It preys upon our strange and unique niche interests and seemingly knows more about us than we know about ourselves. How many times have you been talking about something, and then all of a sudden, it pops up on social media as an ad? Is this convenient or creepy?

The more money I made, the deeper I fell into the trap of mindless browsing and impulsive buying. It felt harmless—everyone else was doing it. We often shop to fill a void or address emotional needs, whether it's to lift our spirits, escape reality, combat boredom, or indulge in a cheap dopamine hit. This behavior, often called "retail therapy," can stem from feelings of sadness, stress, or a craving for instant gratification. We convince ourselves we need these items, but let's be honest—these aren't genuine reasons to buy anything; they're just excuses we cling to while ignoring the deeper issues at play. When we feel unfulfilled in other areas of our lives, shopping provides a temporary escape or boost in mood, but this cycle leads to guilt and dissatisfaction when those purchases don't bring lasting happiness. It's crucial to address the underlying emotions instead of relying on shopping as a coping mechanism. It wasn't until I started to pay close attention to my feelings while I engaged in shopping, that I realized there was rarely any intention present at all. I often felt bored, stressed, or unhappy.

When we buy things carelessly and aimlessly, they lose their significance and value, leaving us feeling worse about our purchases each time. We soon realize that these items didn't bring the happiness we anticipated. Guilt and shame follow, making us feel bad about spending money on things we don't truly value or need. The negative feelings resulting from unintentional shopping drive us to shop again in an attempt to feel better. With each reckless purchase, the dopamine hits harder and stronger, but the pleasure lasts for shorter periods before it wears off more quickly each time. Eventually, we end up having to shop more frequently and to a greater excess to try to satisfy ourselves. Anytime we choose to reach for something external when we're dealing with emotions or stress, instead of facing those feelings head-on, we train our bodies and minds to continue responding this way out of impulse in the future. We have to disrupt this pattern to make any lasting changes.

Obviously, I still like to shop. Though I've drastically cut back and created much more intentional habits, I'm not going to pretend that I don't enjoy it; faking it will not help me long-term. As long as the desire is still there, we'll continue to feel somewhat deprived if we try to fake our feelings around it. Start first by questioning your intentions and asking yourself:

Why do I feel like I need or want something?

What emotional state am I trying to escape from?

Is this purchase going to add real value to my life, or is it just a fleeting impulse?

Will this item contribute to my long-term happiness, or is it simply a momentary distraction?

This introspection will help you get to the root of the reason behind the desire.

One effective way to interrupt this cycle of impulsive purchases is by adding time into the equation and delaying the purchasing process. For example, I'll add something to my cart and then wait about a week to see if that item comes back to my mind. If it doesn't, that's a clear sign I don't need or want it. If it does resurface, I can approach the purchase from a different emotional state—one that isn't tied to the boredom or unhappiness I may have felt when I first added it to my cart. This ensures I'm not training my brain to respond impulsively, seeking a cheap dopamine hit in moments of emotional vulnerability. By delaying the decision, I can make a more rational, clear choice, ultimately leading to greater satisfaction with my purchases and less regret. I know someone's going to be thinking to themselves, "Well, what if the item gets sold out?" If the item ends up being sold out or unavailable in my size by the time I go back to it, then I guess that's just a sign that it wasn't meant to be either. There have been many times that I've gone back to my Amazon cart just to remove items that I previously thought I wanted or needed, only to realize I actually don't.

Establishing clear rules and boundaries around shopping can significantly help minimize impulsive purchases. Consider implementing the following strategies:

- Avoid buying similar items in different colours to prevent unnecessary clutter and wasted money.

- Prioritize second-hand items, which not only saves money but also promote sustainability.

- Shift your focus from material possessions to experiences. Spending money on travel, classes, or events can enrich your life in ways that physical items cannot.

- Create a shopping list before heading out or browsing online, and stick to it to ensure you only purchase what you genuinely need.

- Limit online shopping to specific days of the week to keep unnecessary temptations at bay.

- As mentioned earlier, add time between your purchases.

- Establish a monthly budget for discretionary spending to help limit impulse purchases and keep track of your spending habits.

- Reduce temptation by unsubscribing from retail newsletters and promotional emails that encourage unnecessary spending.

- Recognize your emotional triggers and avoid shopping during times of stress, sadness, or boredom, as this can lead to impulsive purchases.

- After buying something, take a moment to assess its value in your life a few weeks later. This reflection can help reinforce your new shopping habits.

- Invest in quality items that will last. However, do not confuse quality with designer brands. Designer and luxury brands are often emotional purchases that don't necessarily equate to higher quality (more on this in Chapter Seven).

By implementing these rules, you can cultivate a more intentional and fulfilling approach to shopping that aligns with your values and enhances your overall well-being.

There you have it. Those are my personal vices—shopping, alcohol, sugar, and processed foods—that I've been working hard to overcome. As previously mentioned, it is up to you to raise the standards in your own life, and you get to decide which vices have to be eliminated altogether or which ones you'll choose to keep in moderation while implementing healthier boundaries around them. This will vary from person to person, depending on your own morals, values, beliefs, and what you perceive to be problematic or not. Personally, since health and wellness have become a top priority in my life, I choose to eliminate alcohol altogether, substantially cut out processed foods, significantly reduce refined sugars, and limit my shopping to things I either need (like self-care or healthy lifestyle items) or that have been intentionally thought out and purchased from a rational state of mind.

Cultivating the discipline required to maintain these things was not easy at first. However, I can assure you that over time, these eventually become new, healthier habits that will no longer require much effort to sustain. They will become a part of your new life and elevate you toward becoming the best version of yourself possible. They will become your new normal.

An amazing book to help you kick any habit is Alan Carr's *The Easy Way to Stop Smoking*. He has many different books with varying themes based on the same concept, so you can choose whichever one is most appropriate for you. For example, he has versions titled *The Easy Way to Quit Emotional Eating*, *The Easy Way to Control Alcohol* and *Lose Weight Now, The Easy Way*.

As I began to eliminate or drastically reduce my coping mechanisms and vices, I realized for the first time in my life that I was compelled to face my raw feelings and emotions head-on, without the crutch of external distractions. I had to confront reality instead of trying to escape from it. All my feelings of boredom, unfulfillment, inadequacy, social anxiety, and unhappiness bubbled to the surface, as if I were watching my emotions being ground, brewed, extracted, and French-pressed right before my eyes. Through this process, a heart-wrenching truth emerged with clarity—I had to hang up my apron and close the doors of my beloved bakery, marking the end of a chapter that no longer resonated with my true self. This was my first bold, bitter taste of waking up and smelling the coffee.

Take Action: 30-Day Dopamine Detox

Now that we've confronted our vices and unhealthy habits head-on, it's time to take decisive action. Let's commit to a 30-day dopamine detox. A dopamine detox involves temporarily avoiding all things that provide any type of instant gratification (or instant dopamine hits). This includes social media, video games, junk food, alcohol, gambling, sugar, binge-watching TV, shopping, and anything else you personally partake in along those lines.

The idea behind abstaining from these activities for a set period of time is to reset our brain's reward system by reducing the overexposure to dopamine triggers. When we overindulge in cheap, quick dopamine hits, we train our brains to become less sensitized to them over time, leading us to seek even greater hits to feel similar levels of satisfaction in the future. Think about how unsustainable this is if we continue this behaviour recklessly without intervention. After completing the 30-day dopamine detox, you should feel improved levels of productivity, focus, enjoyment, and overall well-being. I bet that after 30 days, you'll feel so good that you won't even want to return to many of your old habits.

Here's How to Get Started:

1. **Make a List**: Write down all the activities you currently engage in that provide instant dopamine hits.

2. **Commit to a Month**: Decide to abstain from these activities for a full 30 days.

3. **Replace Old Habits**: Use the time you would have spent on these activities to engage in healthier alternatives, such as:

- **Exercise**: Go for a run, join a fitness class, or practice yoga.

- **Spend Time Outdoors**: Enjoy nature through hiking, walking, or simply relaxing outside.

- **Reading**: Dive into books that interest you or explore new genres.

- **Learn a New Hobby**: Take up painting, cooking, or playing a musical instrument.

- **Spend Time with People in Person**: Connect with friends and family face-to-face to foster meaningful relationships.

- **Volunteering**: Get involved in your community and help others, which can provide a sense of fulfilment.

At first, you might feel bored, anxious, or irritated, but I promise that the long-term benefits outweigh the short-term discomfort. Though these alternative activities also produce dopamine, they do so in a more gradual, stabilized way, leading to long-term fulfilment and satisfaction rather than short-term dependency.

If you have kids, I highly encourage you to get them on this detox as well. Research shows that children and adolescents are particularly vulnerable to the effects of dopamine and instant gratification. For example, a study published in the journal *Nature* found that excessive exposure to instant gratification can lead to impulsive behaviour and lower academic performance in young people. You can implement this detox without them even knowing by simply replacing any of their cheap dopamine habits with healthier alternatives. Their developing brains are much more sensitive and susceptible to the long-term consequences of cheap dopamine addiction early on, as evidenced by research in *Psychological Science* that highlights how early exposure to high-reward environments can impact brain development and decision-making in children.

Imagine a life where satisfaction comes from intentional experiences rather than fleeting pleasures. This transformation may bring discomfort, but each small victory propels you closer to the best version of yourself. Let this chapter ignite your journey, inspiring you to rise above old patterns and embrace a future brimming with fulfilment.

Chapter Five

FORGET FEAR AND GO WITH THE FLOW—NO ONE CARES ANYWAY

The only thing more terrifying than realizing that you need to make a major change in your life is the act of actually making that change. The soul knows when it's time to move on from something long before we allow our minds to make sense of it. As humans, we've evolved to make decisions based on logic and what is rational, instead of trusting our intuition. The universe isn't as rational and logical as the human mind would like for us to believe that it is. Long before our brains evolved to think logically and rationally, trusting our intuition and instincts was all that we knew how to do. Somewhere along the line—with the evolution of modern society—we developed the skills to think logically and rationally. This sense of rationality and mental control gives us the illusion that we're safe and secure. But how safe and secure are we really? We are born, and then we die. In between birth and death lies a whole lot of unsafety and insecurity, considering that we could die at any moment. And yet, we still try to dictate so much of our lives, ignoring the obvious elephant in the room—that we aren't going to live forever (though our minds would love for us to believe that we might). In fact, as each moment passes and the seconds tick by, we're all becoming closer and closer to death. So why do we live our lives as if we have unlimited amounts of time?

Take a moment to pause and reflect on this question.

I want this chapter to awaken your spirit and soul to the reality of time. Recognizing the importance of time and the fragility of life is essential. If you continue to believe that you're guaranteed tomorrow, you will lack the courage to make meaningful changes in your life today. How many times have you negotiated with yourself to start something in the future? "I'll start my diet on Monday," or "I'll start looking for a new job next month," or "Next year is when I'll start doing..." These are all negotiations we make with ourselves to feel content in the moment by deferring what we know we should start doing right now. If we were really serious about something, we would start today—right now. Rather than wasting time making excuses for why we can't start right now, we should concentrate on finding solutions and eliminating obstacles in our path. We often fall into these deceptive negotiations with ourselves because they create a false sense of progress and offer temporary satisfaction, even if we haven't taken any meaningful action.

Another reason why we create excuses for not being able to make changes immediately is that we aren't really that serious about the change in the first place. We don't want it bad enough. Even if we know we really should do something, unless it becomes a must-do, chances are that we will continue to create excuses and reasons why we can't do it. I've learned that it's better to recognize this pattern of behaviour and just be honest with myself when I start to fall into this negative spiral. I hold myself accountable. Instead of saying I will start something on a future date, I just tell myself that it is not a priority in my life right now. If it were, then I would start doing it today. Being brutally honest with myself has built a lot of trust in my own abilities. I'm not constantly breaking promises to myself by saying I'll start something on a future date, only to not follow through on those promises. Feeling the sting and discomfort of our own brutal honesty can often be exactly what we need in order to find the courage to successfully implement major changes. Breaking promises to ourselves is the fastest way to diminish our self-confidence. Conversely, keeping promises to ourselves is the quickest way to build it. In my previous book, *The Million Dollar Bakery*, I mentioned that confidence doesn't mean having all the answers but rather trusting in your own ability to figure things out.

How confident would you be in a relationship or friendship where someone said one thing only to never follow through? Not very confident. The relationship with yourself is no different. You have to build trust in your own abilities to follow through, figure things out, and act on what you say you're going to do. Otherwise, just be honest and say you don't actually want to do it. The most important relationship you'll ever have is with yourself. Hold yourself accountable the same way you'd expect to hold a friend or a partner accountable.

We all have a dream in our hearts, and it's there for a reason. Some people may be more aware of their dream than others, and sometimes discovering what that dream is will require us to say no to everything that the dream definitely is not. If you can't clearly identify your dream, you need to start by creating space in your life to allow it to reveal itself to you. More on this in Chapter Six. Being busy with tedious tasks, never-ending to-do lists, and un-fulfilling job duties will ensure you never discover or act upon your dreams. When you're not on the right path to pursuing that dream, you'll physically be able to feel the unalignment within yourself if you take a moment to pause and reflect. Unalignment in our lives shows up disguised as many different feelings, such as discomfort, anxiety, dread, boredom, being uninspired, lack of joy, feeling depressed, and experiencing a sense of monotony. Pay close attention to the discomfort that you're feeling because it is trying to get your attention in order to realign you with your life's purpose. The more we choose to ignore that dream in our hearts and opt for safety, security, and rationalization, the more miserable we'll be. Personally, it becomes painful and annoying as hell to continue relearning the same lessons over and over again when I'm being stubborn and refusing to pay attention to the signs of redirection. Running into the same situations and problems should be a clear indi-cator that you need to head in a different direction to get a different result. The Universe has a mischievous way of putting the same types of people, problems, and situations in our lives until we start making different choices to prove that we've learned our lessons. That's exactly what will happen to you if you choose to ignore the signs that the Universe is sending you as you attempt to control your circumstances. It will drive you absolutely nuts. Maybe it already has been? The only reason we tend to ignore these intuitive feelings is that we logically try to convince ourselves that staying where we're at is safer, more secure, and "makes more sense." Talk about an oxymoron. Nothing about human existence really makes much sense when you think about it fundamentally. We are creatures living on a giant pile of dirt, suspended in a galaxy among planets and stars. Once you gain perspective on how illogical and irrational it sounds when you think about it literally, you'll realize that perhaps following the dream in your heart doesn't need to make too much sense after all. Consider what it would look like to embrace your dreams rather than overthink them. Stop resisting it. Stop trying to understand it. Stop rationalizing it. Start making room for it, and most importantly, start to pursue it.

I started feeling the nudge of unalignment in my business years before I wanted to admit it to myself. It scared me because I had invested all my time, energy, and money into starting and growing my bakery business from the ground up. I didn't realize that my attempts to understand and intellectualize my feelings didn't actually matter; instead, I had to learn to accept the feelings and allow it to guide me in a different direction. It was the fear of what the new direction would be like that kept me from acting on my intuitive feelings. So, I stayed stuck for a few years, knowing in my heart that I needed to move on, but my head was resisting the urge. I did what most people do when they're feeling stuck in a job, career, business, or relationship that they know is no longer serving them—I suppressed it, ignored it, and downright avoided it. I used vices like wine, shopping, and comfort food to soothe the discomfort and provide the much-needed dopamine hits that I was lacking in my daily life. I promised myself that someday I would be able to move on and close this chapter in my life, but it seemed irresponsible to do it right now. I made myself feel guilty for not being grateful for this successful business that I had created and how ridiculous it seemed to just close it down. Between all the back-and-forth thoughts going through my head and the Universe serving me signs on a silver platter, I eventually gave in to the truth—it didn't matter what I thought about any of it. I couldn't out-logic my own intuition. Doing so made me feel like I was paddling upstream through raging rapids with a fork as a paddle. Eventually, I came to terms with the fact that I knew in my heart it was time to close down my business and create space in my life for more aligned opportunities to present themselves.

The Wisdom of Wu Wei

As humans, we always want to have some kind of "plan" to feel safe and in control of our destiny, and I was no exception. This time, however, I had no plan. I only knew the direction I needed to head toward. So, I decided to take a different approach and trust that, as Gabby Bernstein would say, "The Universe had my back."

I read several books and watched many YouTube videos on how to go with the flow and embrace trust in the universe, and I came across something called Wu Wei. When translated literally, Wu Wei means "inaction" or "effortless action." The objective of living a Wu Wei lifestyle is to find peace and harmony in the flow of the natural universe and to allow things to unfold around us naturally.

It's about learning how to stop controlling and dictating outcomes. This concept has completely changed my life from being a control freak and an over-planner to learning how to effortlessly go with the flow of life. Growing up in our Western culture, where the opposite of Wu Wei had been ingrained in my psyche—working hard, controlling my destiny, and hustling—it felt as if my perspective had been flipped upside down. Understanding Wu Wei was a challenge to wrap my head around, and implementing it felt impossible at first. It took a lot of research, reinforcement, and plenty of practice to gain even the slightest momentum with it. Not only was it about learning the foundations of Wu Wei, but it was equally about unlearning the Western culture's hustle mentality. Naturally, as someone who grew up conditioned by a capitalistic culture in the Western world, Wu Wei sounded to me like an excuse to be unfocused, undetermined, and just plain lazy.

Having already lived thirty-plus years with the Western mentality (and witnessing the stress and chaos that it entailed), I was ready to open my mind to this new Wu Wei of thinking, regardless of how bizarre it sounded. I learned that Wu Wei doesn't mean completely giving up on taking action altogether; instead, it means taking action in an easy and effortless way without being attached to the external outcome. In our Western society, almost everything we do is attached to an external outcome. An external outcome is a result that depends on factors outside of our control, often measured by societal standards, validation from others, or achievements rather than personal fulfilment. Nothing feels more liberating than letting go of external outcomes and personal rewards, and embracing situations as they are rather than clinging to what we wish they could be. It's always our own expectations that end up causing disappointment, not the actual situations themselves. Funny how we are more prone to blaming external situations than we are to accepting personal responsibility for our unmet expectations. Living in peace and harmony with Wu Wei has allowed me to embrace my journey without the need to control my destiny or know what's next. Instead, it has enabled me to relax and enjoy the process of the Universe presenting me with opportunities that it knows are aligned with my life's purpose. There are so many great books, podcasts, and videos on Wu Wei that can teach you all about this beautiful philosophy, and I encourage you to start tuning in to them to learn more.

To kick-start your Wu Wei journey, take a moment to pause and identify a situation in your life where you currently feel pressure to control the outcome. Instead of forcing things to happen, try to step back and let things unfold naturally. This week, practice saying "I'm open to possibilities" whenever faced with a decision, big or small. Allow yourself to trust your intuition rather than overthinking. These small shifts will help you embrace the flow and discover the ease of living in alignment with yourself.

Freedom from Others' Opinions

This chapter is all about leaving fear behind and developing the courage to admit which areas of your life are not aligned with you so that you can let them go and make room for what is. A big part of leaving fear behind is ridding yourself of the fear of other people's opinions. I don't care how badass you are or how tough you think it sounds to not care what anyone else thinks about you; we are all wired to care to some degree. It's actually an ancestral desire to fit in with a tribe (or a community, as we call it these days). Our core human needs are to feel loved, seen, and heard, and these cannot be fulfilled without caring, to some extent, about what others think.

Here's a little secret: it is possible to care about what others think in a way that does not allow their thoughts and opinions to impede or devalue our own. Other people's thoughts, opinions, and beliefs come from their personal perspectives and really have nothing to do with you, me, or anyone else. Sometimes perspectives from others can help us see things from different angles and gain further valuable insight into situations, which can be helpful, but that's about all they're good for. We run into problems when we compromise our own values and feelings to appease someone else. For example, imagine your career no longer aligns with your true self, and you feel deep down that it's time to move on. When you share this with a friend, they will process your feelings through their own experiences. Their perspective is heavily influenced by their own baggage and insecurities. They also aren't experiencing the emotional pull that drives your desire for change. As a result, you receive advice that sounds somewhat valid but is rooted in their own fear and lack of passion. They might say something like, "I wouldn't do that if I were you. I'd prefer the financial security of staying at my current job. What if it doesn't work out?" This response reflects their circumstances, beliefs, and insecurities rather than what's best for you. Opinions from others may seem reasonable and factual, but it's important to remember that they stem from their own perspectives. No one can truly know what's best for you, except for you.

Another point about others' opinions is that they often concentrate on the negatives; for instance, they might say, "What if it doesn't work out?" This question usually comes from a place of love because, by making you think twice about your decision, they feel less responsible for the outcome. What if they encouraged you and you ended up failing? Our friends and family don't want to feel responsible for encouraging things that have even the slightest chance of failure because it would make them feel bad. It's easier for them to play it safe and give advice that points out and prevents any possible negative outcomes or opportunities to fail. The problem is that playing it safe and not failing will not get anyone closer to fulfilling their life's purpose. Failing is part of every process in life. If you stay at your current job, you will fail at something, and if you change to a new job, you will fail at something there too. Failure is a critical part of the path to success. It's part of every evolution process, and it's something to embrace, not fear. It's certainly not something to allow to hold you back. Personally, I'm less interested in knowing what would happen if you failed and more interested in knowing what would happen if you succeeded. People who recognize that failure is a crucial aspect of growth and embrace their own setbacks are often the ones who will inspire you to take risks and highlight the advantages of your success.

Since it would be unrealistic to not care at all about other people's opinions, I encourage you to simply start caring less about them. Start by being selective regarding whom you seek advice from; only ask people whose opinions you actually value and trust. I also avoid seeking advice from people who aren't where you'd want to be. For example, if your best friend is constantly complaining about her marriage, you wouldn't want to ask her for relationship advice. Similarly, if you have a friend who has been stuck in a dead-end job that they hate, they're probably not the best person to consult about starting your own business and chasing your dreams. Knowing whom to seek advice from will help you avoid cluttering your mind with the opinions of people you'd never want to become anyway. Always aim to seek guidance from those who embody the success you aspire to achieve. Ultimately, you should always draw your own conclusions, regardless of how much you respect someone else's input. I learned to always allow my heart and intuition to have the final say.

No One Fucking Cares

While it might feel like the weight of the world is on your shoulders when faced with making a big decision, I'll let you in on a little secret that will instantly release all the pressure… No one *actually* cares. Or, as my husband often hears me say very enthusiastically, "No one fucking cares!" Initially, it might make you feel sad to hear this, but I'll tell you something. When I realized this, I was so deeply relieved that it wasn't even funny. It's as if the weight of the world was pricked with the sharpest needle and deflated instantaneously, in cohesion with a sigh of relief being expelled from my lungs. Even the people who support and care about you don't actually really care what you do. The only time anyone will actually care what you're doing is if it directly affects them. Human nature is inherently selfish.

For most of my adult life, I believed that everyone cared what I did, said, didn't do, or didn't say. It felt like everyone was watching my every move, judging me the entire time. Social media only exacerbated the problem, creating immense pressure to respond to every DM, text message, and email that vied for my attention. I had anxiety about how often I needed to show up on social media so that my followers didn't feel neglected. I'd become burdened by my self-imposed to-do list, which seemed to reproduce tasks out of nowhere, as if it were a Mary Poppins bag of never-ending tasks. All of this extra energy I was spending worrying about what I was doing (or not doing) and what other people thought about what I was doing (or not doing) was exhausting, making it impossible to keep up with and even more miserable to try and maintain. I've since learned that the pressure that we feel from these perceived obligations comes directly from our ego. It comes from thinking that we are so important that everyone around us cares deeply about what we are doing (or not doing). Our egoic imagination will lead us to believe that our friends, family, followers, and acquaintances cannot carry on with their own lives without our influence.

Social media has conned many of us into believing that our followers can't get through their days without us actively engaging with them daily. I'll talk more in depth about social media in Chapter Nine. It's an important realization to recognize that no one actually cares how often you show up, what your Instagram grid looks like, how bad your hair looks in that selfie, or how long of a break you took away from social media. No one cares because everyone's lives are continuing on as normal, regardless of how often you show up or how instantly you respond. In fact, it's highly likely that amidst the clutter and content on social media these days, no one even notices your engagement level at all. Everyone is struggling to keep up with their own lives and is too busy juggling their own hectic schedules to keep up with or concern themselves with yours. It's the truth.

I remember one time during a therapy session, when I was in the hustle and grind of growing my business, I told my therapist how overwhelmed I felt with the amount of emails and DMs I always had to respond to. As an introvert, social interactions of any kind can overstimulate me pretty quickly.

To which she replied, "Well, why do you even feel the obligation to respond to them all?"

I didn't know what she meant by that and I remember saying something like, "What do you mean? Like, not respond to them at all?"

She replied, with that being exactly what she meant. I had never even considered that I had a choice in the matter. She continued to tell me that no response was actually, in fact, a response in and of itself and asked me, "What's the worst that could happen if you don't respond?"

"I don't know. I guess they won't email me again," I said.

"Problem solved," she replied.

Perplexed by the simplicity of what felt like should have been an obvious observation, I smirked. Touché.

Of course, if you have a business and are trying to grow or increase sales, then appointing someone to respond to all emails and DMs is just smart business sense, but otherwise... who cares?

Since then, I've learned that if someone's email or DM isn't interesting or exciting, why would I waste my energy responding to it? If I am genuinely interested and excited to reply, I will feel inclined to do so immediately. But if it doesn't capture my interest, why waste time and energy responding at all? I understand that it can feel rude or impolite to ignore people, but if the trade-off is that you're responding at the expense of your own energy and wellbeing, then it's never worth it. Our time and energy are precious, and we are the only ones responsible for reserving these non-renewable resources for what truly matters. We must protect them from anything—and anyone—that doesn't.

The Spotlight Effect

Establishing healthy boundaries for communication and time management is tough in an age where social media, instant messaging, and emails are constantly vying for our attention. It wasn't until I learned about the Spotlight Effect that I was able to fully let go of my self-imposed sense of responsibility. According to Wikipedia, the Spotlight Effect is defined as follows: "The spotlight effect is the psychological phenomenon by which people tend to believe they are being noticed more than they really are, being that one is constantly in the centre of one's own world. The reason for the spotlight effect is the innate tendency to forget that although one is the centre of one's own world, one is not the centre of everyone else's."

In other words, no one really cares about you as much as your ego would like for you to believe that they do. It's called the spotlight effect because it feels as though there is a permanent spotlight on you and that you're constantly being observed, giving you the false illusion that people care when they don't.

Social media has the ability to significantly amplify the spotlight effect because we tend to share so much of our lives online and expect others to notice or care about everything that we post. The reality is that unless your content adds value to them, benefits them in some way, or triggers them negatively, they likely won't engage, notice, or care. The spotlight effect shows up in many different ways, both online and in real life. Some examples of when you might feel this effect happening in your own life could be:

1. **Physical Appearance**: Let's say that you decide to wear a new outfit that's very different from what you would normally wear. You feel self-conscious and like people are going to stare and judge you when, in reality, they don't even notice anything different about you. Maybe you changed your hairstyle and got bangs for the first time in years, but feel like it draws negative attention to a mole near your forehead, and you worry that people will notice or comment on it. Other people often don't care or no-

tice things about ourselves that don't have anything
to do with them.

2. **Weaknesses and Flaws**: Even though you might be
   self-conscious about your own personal flaws and
   weaknesses, it doesn't mean anyone else notices
   them. It can feel embarrassing if you're not fluent in
   a second language that you're trying to learn how to
   speak, and you feel like everyone is judging you for
   how badly you sound and how often you stumble
   on your words. In reality, they probably expect you
   to stumble a bit and acknowledge the difficulty of
   learning a second language. Chances are that they
   actually think more highly of you for even attempting to learn a second language at all.

3. **Mistakes**: In the spotlight effect world, there's little
   more embarrassing than making a glaringly obvious mistake in front of someone else. God forbid
   someone else sees your humanity and judges you
   for it. First of all, who cares what they think of
   you making a mistake? Second of all, we all make
   mistakes. Period.

4. **Achievements**: Even some positive situations can
   lead to a false sense of importance with the spotlight effect. You might share something with someone that you expect them to celebrate you for, only
   to find out that they don't really care that much
   about your achievements. Things like receiving an
   award or running a marathon might be big achievements for you personally; however, they're not a

big deal to anyone else. It might leave you feeling down about your achievements when you accomplish something, only to find out that no one really commented on it or went out of their way to congratulate you. Even the people who do take a second to offer their congratulations don't care as much as you think they do, I promise. This is why it's so important to detach ourselves from external outcomes and refocus on what matters most—how we feel internally.

5. **Social Events**: Imagine attending a party where you feel like everyone is judging your social skills or how well you're interacting with others. You might think that people are closely observing whether you're having fun or fitting in. In reality, most guests are preoccupied with their own conversations and interactions, often not paying attention to you at all.

6. **Public Speaking**: When giving a presentation or speaking in front of a group, it's common to feel like all eyes are on you, scrutinizing every word and movement. However, the audience is typically focused on the content of your presentation and the value it's offering them, rather than critiquing your delivery. Many people in the audience may even empathize with your nerves, recalling their own experiences of speaking in public.

7. **Fitness**: If you start a new workout routine or attend a fitness class, you might worry that others are judging your fitness level or how you look while

exercising. In truth, most people are concentrated on their own workouts and personal goals, and they likely don't even notice how shitty your squat form is.

I consider myself to be a pretty caring person in general, and I'm sure that you do too. But think about this: Do you really care that much about someone you went to high school with who posted on Facebook about their kid losing their first tooth and earning their first dollar from the tooth fairy? No! Why would you? If it weren't for Facebook, we'd never even have thought about it. It's not that you or I don't care about anyone entirely... Most humans are wired to care about the well-being of other humans; it's just not to the extent that we've been conditioned to believe. If we're being honest, we only genuinely care about people's overall well-being and health; beyond that, not much else truly matters to us. When we can admit how little we care about the nuances of other people's lives, then we should also be able to understand why we needn't expect others to care deeply about our own.

Naturally, our closest friends and family are likely to care a bit more about the details of our lives compared to acquaintances or strangers. However, even their level of concern is usually not as intense as we might believe. Short of caring about you being healthy and happy, don't expect people to care too deeply about what's going on in your life and the decisions you're making. The further outside of your closest friends and family circle, the less and less you can expect anyone to care unless, as I mentioned earlier, it benefits them (or triggers them) in some way. Social media creates a misleading illusion of having numerous followers and acquaintances who "like" our posts and "comment" as if they genuinely care about our lives, but in reality, this engagement is often quite superficial. Once I realized that no one truly cares about my choices, actions, preferences, achievements, or anything else. I felt a newfound freedom to pursue what I wanted without seeking validation or approval. I began living authentically, embracing who I truly am without any apologies. I hope you'll find the same sense of freedom after reading this chapter.

As we grow and evolve, it's essential to regularly take the time to reevaluate and check in with ourselves to ensure we're still on the right path. You might be surprised at how frequently we continue doing things we've outgrown simply out of habit. Time is ticking, and your life is happening right now. The more attuned you are to your gut feelings, intuition, and emotions, the faster you'll recognize when you're straying off course and can realign yourself. We aren't meant to remain in one place indefinitely; instead, we should learn from our experiences and keep progressing through life, gaining new skills and knowledge that allow us to transition into different stages of our journey. The unhappiest individuals are often those who remain unchanged since high school, continuing to engage in the same activities, socialize with the same friends, and maintain the same mindset, lacking any growth or development. We all know people like that, where the only thing that's changed about them is their age and appearance. These are the people who aren't in tune with their life's purpose or dreams. They end up sleepwalking through their lives and wonder what the point was. Don't let that be you.

I'm encouraging you to leave fear behind, discard other people's opinions, get rid of the illusory spotlight, and dig deep within yourself to answer these questions:

What do I need to let go of in my life right now in order to make room for something better?

What do I need to add more of in my life right now in order to feel more passionate, energized, and alive?

What would I do differently if I were not concerned about others' opinions?

What are some moments where I thought people were focused on me, but later realized they weren't?

How can I remind myself that everyone has their own insecurities and is often focused on themselves rather than judging me?

Chapter Six

Committing to a New Path and Discovering Your Gift

What is your gift?

What a simple yet complicated question. The only reason that it feels complicated is that we, as humans, overcomplicate it. It doesn't need to be that challenging. After reading through the last chapter, we've been able to shed a lot of the burdens that we've acquired from our social conditioning. Getting rid of expectations from others and any old beliefs we've acquired throughout the years that have been holding us back from living our most authentic lives is imperative. If we don't know who we are or what our purpose is in this life, then we end up letting society decide for us. Society doesn't care about our gifts, purpose, or whether or not we're living in alignment with who we really are. Society's main concern is its economic functionality. As long as we're working and producing something beneficial, it won't care if you feel burdened, unhappy, unfulfilled, and dread every second of every day that you wake up. Society will be happy to have you working tirelessly on the production line, creating products and generating profits while you sell your soul for a dollar.

Ironically, our society would be much better off if more people in the world chose to honour and embrace their gifts. It would raise our collective vibration and result in a happier, healthier population of people. Who wouldn't benefit from living in a society filled with people like that? It sounds like heaven on earth to me. The reality is that many of our modern-day industries wouldn't benefit from such a society, as they thrive on a workforce that is driven by profit rather than passion. This is alarming to say the least and one of the biggest, brightest, boldest red flags that's ever flown.

One of my favourite quotes that I've heard came from Steve Harvey, who said, "Embrace your gift and God will make room for you." It originated from a biblical scripture, and though I'm not overly religious, I found so much power in this quote. I highly recommend watching Steve's video speech on this topic, available on YouTube. It is so powerful and inspiring. The premise is that we are all given gifts from God, and it is our responsibility to discover what our gift is and to fully embrace and utilize it to its fullest potential. Only when we start using our gift and aligning our careers, relationships, and hobbies with it will we find true happiness, success, and fulfilment in life. The line where it says, "God will make room for you," implies that you don't necessarily have to know exactly which direction to go in; all you need to do is identify and actively engage in activities that align with your gift and let God (or the Universe) take care of providing the opportunities for you. I love this so much because living a life rooted in our gifts sounds incredibly fulfilling. It's also reassuring to know that we don't have to determine the specific path or details; we can trust God (or the Universe) to guide us in the right direction. This also aligns with the Wu Wei concept of going with the flow, which encourages us to embrace the natural course of life. In this chapter, I want you to discover your gift, and I'm here to help you do just that. While it's often straightforward to identify the activities we enjoy, broadening our perspective can sometimes be necessary to uncover the overarching theme of our gift. For me, that gift is creativity. I am an artist, and there are countless ways I can express and utilize this gift. My favourite creative outlets include writing, photography, videography, painting, and almost any other form of art. As long as I pursue creativity in my life in some capacity, I trust that God will provide me with the opportunities to grow and flourish.

As humans, we also vibrate at a higher frequency when we're engaged in our gifts, and therefore, we'll be able to attract higher vibrational opportunities and greater success to us. Vibrating at a higher frequency means operating with a sense of joy, purpose, and positivity, which in turn, draws experiences, people, and situations that align with our best selves. It's no wonder that I was able to create such an abnormally successful bakery business. It wasn't the baking or the business itself that made it successful—it was the result of me using my gift to create extremely creative and artistic desserts and serve others with it. If your gift is creativity, seek out a career that allows you to use that talent regularly. This could be in fields like digital design, marketing, working in an art museum or art supply shop, teaching art classes, hair styling, makeup artistry, art therapy, and more. Steer clear of careers that lack creativity. Even if it means taking a short-term pay cut, aligning yourself with a role that taps into your gift will open the door to bigger and better opportunities down the line. You'll also be pleasantly surprised by the boost in energy and happiness you experience when you embrace your gift, making every aspect of your life feel more fulfilling.

When trying to determine your gift, reflect on what you love to do. Consider the activities where time seems to fly by, and you find yourself fully immersed in the task at hand. These moments often provide the best clues about your true gifts. Pay attention to the emotions you experience during these activities; feelings of joy, excitement, or fulfilment usually signal alignment with your natural talents. Also, think about how these activities make you feel afterward—if they leave you energized and inspired, they likely reflect your unique abilities. For example, if you feel this way about physical activity, your gift may lie in athleticism. This could lead you to careers such as a personal trainer, working at a gym, fitness instructor, or coach, among many other options. Gifts come in many forms, each reflecting the unique talents and passions we possess. Some individuals have a gift for communication, effortlessly connecting with others through spoken or written words, making them excellent teachers, speakers, or writers. Others may possess analytical thinking skills, enabling them to solve complex problems and interpret intricate data—qualities that are invaluable in fields like science, engineering, and finance. Some shine through their empathy and emotional intelligence, naturally understanding and supporting others, making them exceptional counselors, therapists, nurses, personal support workers or social workers. Recognizing the diverse range of gifts not only broadens our understanding of them but also encourages us to appreciate our unique contributions to the world.

If you're uncertain about what your gift might be, a powerful exercise is to consider the activities that you would willingly engage in for free, without any expectation of payment or reward. This reflection allows you to tap into your intrinsic motivations and interests, shedding the constraints and pressures that often accompany financial considerations. When we remove monetary rewards from the equation, we create space for genuine exploration of our passions. It encourages us to think about what truly excites us, what brings us joy, and what makes us lose track of time. This approach can reveal insights into our authentic selves. Once we uncover our gifts, we can then brainstorm creative ways to monetize them and turn them into a meaningful career.

If you're still struggling to identify your gift, consider asking some of your closest friends what they notice you're good at. Often, those who know you well can provide valuable insights that you might overlook. Reflecting on your childhood can also be illuminating; think about the activities that brought you joy back then and made you lose track of time. This is one of the easiest ways to identify your gift, as childhood interests often reveal our innate passions and talents. Additionally, consider the moments in your life when you felt most alive and engaged. Pay attention to the activities that energize you and make you feel fulfilled. Together, these clues can guide you toward discovering your unique gift and purpose.

Once you begin to uncover your true talents, it's essential to shift your perspective on work. We need to redefine what work means. We've been heavily influenced and conditioned by society and school to focus on what seems "realistic," and we're taught that work should feel "hard." It's a lie. Work should feel meaningful, and it should be enjoyable. It should challenge and stimulate us, but not feel constantly draining and difficult. When we align our work with our passions and strengths, it becomes a source of joy rather than a burden. This shift in mindset allows us to view work as an opportunity for growth and fulfilment, fostering creativity and productivity. Embracing this perspective can lead to a more balanced life where work contributes to our overall happiness and well-being rather than detracting from it.

Something I learned the hard way with my bakery business is that as it grew, I ended up using my gift of creativity less and less. The demands of the business side of things became so overwhelming that they consumed the majority of my time, leaving me primarily performing business tasks. Before I knew it, I was no longer engaged in anything creative, and the business I'd built based on my creativity was no longer utilizing my gift. I didn't realize any of this while building my business. How could I? I was too busy. I became so caught up in the daily operations and growth goals that I didn't take any time to consider where I was headed or whether I was still aligned with my gift as the business grew.

This is a struggle most small business owners and entrepreneurs will face, often leading to burnout and misery at some point. Being a business owner may align with someone's gifts if they love networking, marketing, sales, HR, and can solve problems analytically. However, as explained in Chapter One, many small businesses are started by individuals whose true gift isn't running a business, but rather creating a product or providing a specific service. When we stop utilizing our gifts within the business and shift our focus to being a business owner, we often move away from the very thing that inspired us to start our businesses in the first place. This is exactly what happened with my business, too. I started it as a hobby, just for fun, baking and decorating extremely elaborate and creative desserts for family and friends. I decided to turn this hobby into a business and eventually grew it to four store locations with a fleet of delivery vehicles that serviced a two-hour radius. I scaled it to over a million dollars in yearly revenue, which led me to hire others to handle the part I loved—creating the products—while I stepped into a CEO role. I went from utilizing my gift of art and creativity every single day (and loving it) to taking on a completely different set of job duties that had nothing to do with my gift of creativity or what I loved to do. The scariest part of all was that I didn't even notice it happening.

Your journey as a business owner doesn't have to mirror my experience; I'm sharing my story to help you avoid the pitfalls that come from straying too far from your passion. If you're a business owner who started your venture as a hobby—creating cool products or providing a skilled service—now is a great time to check in with yourself and see if what you're doing is still aligned with your gift. Regular self-reflection is crucial; it ensures you remain true to your passions and adapt as necessary. This applies not only to business owners but to anyone with a job or corporate career too. Let's say your gift is in sales. You love the company that you work for and believe wholeheartedly in the product or service you're selling. You enjoy connecting and building relationships with potential clients all day, but then you accept a promotion to become a manager instead. It's still within the same company, but all of a sudden, instead of using your gift of selling every day, you're managing, scheduling, training, and doing tasks that are completely unaligned with your strengths. Recognizing this shift early can prevent you from spiralling into feelings of frustration and disengagement, allowing you to quickly realign yourself with your talents. Be aware that promotions and wage increases can often cloud our judgment. It's important to stay true to who you are, what you love, and use your gift to its fullest potential.

The best way to put our gifts to practical use is to figure out how we can use it to serve others. Serving others while utilizing our gifts is a match made in heaven. I believe this is the real reason we were all given different and unique gifts in the first place: to share them with our communities and enhance the lives of others. Our ancestors did this back in the day by cultivating a tribe where everyone would use their own gifts and skills to hunt, gather, and create things. Then they would trade with each other so that everyone could benefit and have what they needed. If they all just utilized their own gifts without sharing them with others, they would've ended up with a lot of one thing—perhaps an abundance of food—but then no water, shelter, clothing, or tools. We also don't find as much joy or fulfilment when we engage in our gift alone without sharing it with others. Experiencing the joy that our gift brings someone else is the ultimate reward. Why would an artist paint a beautiful piece of art and keep it locked away in their room for no one else to see or enjoy? As mentioned in Chapter Three—The Science of Happiness, when we add people to share an experience with us, it makes the experience memorable and meaningful. Take this as an opportunity to uncover your gift and brainstorm all the different ways you can start engaging in it regularly today. The more often you can utilize it, the better. Look for career and volunteer opportunities, as well as hobbies, that allow you to share your gifts and positively impact the lives of others.

A Step-by-Step Guide to Identifying Your Gift and Re-aligning Your Career

1. **Self-Reflection**: Identify activities that energize you and make you lose track of time.

2. **Gather Feedback**: Ask friends and family about your strengths.

3. **Shadow Professionals**: Spend a day observing individuals in different careers to understand their daily tasks.

4. **Informational Interviews**: Schedule one-on-one chats with individuals in your desired career to gain insights and advice.

5. **Experiment**: Try workshops, volunteer opportunities, or side projects related to your gifts.

6. **Research Careers**: Investigate fields that align with your gifts and connect with professionals.

7. **Create a Career Vision Board**: Visually map out your gifts and aspirations using images and words that inspire you.

8. **Create a Plan**: Outline steps for transitioning to a new career, including short and long-term goals.

9. **Take Action**: Update your resume and apply for suitable positions.

10. **Reflect**: Regularly assess if your role aligns with your gifts and adjust as needed.

This action plan will help you identify your gifts and guide you toward finding a fulfilling career. Remember, the journey of self-discovery is ongoing; stay open to new experiences and insights as you explore your path. Embrace the process, and know that by aligning your career with your unique gifts, you'll not only enhance your own life but also positively impact those around you. Your gifts are meant to be shared—let them shine in every aspect of your work.

Chapter Seven

DETACHMENT—LOVING PEOPLE AND USING THINGS

Nothing has changed my life and shifted my perspective quite like learning how to detach myself from material things. Learning the concept of loving people, not things, and using things, not people (something I learned from The Minimalists, who have a book with that very title) has forever shifted my relationship with both people and things. Though I've never cared much for ultra-luxurious designer brands or super boujee fashion trends (I never understood the point), I will admit that I had a pretty healthy appetite for material things in general. As previously mentioned in Chapter Four, I used shopping as one of my vices of choice. I had the "work hard, play hard" mentality down to a science, and while it was admittedly a fun thrill for a bit, the novelty eventually wore off. Being born and raised in a Western capitalist culture, I'd never heard of the idea of detachment before. Actually, it's something I just learned about recently as I delved into some spiritual books that opened my mind and heart to a whole new world and way of being. When I talk about detachment, I'm referring to its definition in Buddhist teachings specifically, which defines it as: "Non-attachment, also known as detachment or non-clinging, is a key concept in Buddhism that refers to the practice of letting go of attachment to material possessions, desires, and emotions in order to achieve inner peace and enlightenment."

Yikes—I don't know about you, but that sounded like some really far-out shit to me. To be completely honest, I thought it sounded like something someone would say who has given up on life and was pretending to try to make themselves feel better for being broke and having nothing. How could someone genuinely be content with letting go of their material things? What was the point of working so hard if not to buy things with the money we were earning? These were all the thoughts racing through my mind when I'd first heard of this concept. It's in complete opposition to the way that the majority of us grew up here in our Western culture. The concept of Buddhist detachment also involves letting go of expectations, desires, and emotions—each equally important. In this chapter, I want to focus specifically on detaching from material things. By developing a healthier relationship with the material world, we can also alleviate many of our desires, expectations, and emotions in the process. I hope to inspire you to fully embrace the idea of detachment so that you can start to experience the benefits for yourself.

Before we dive into my explanation and tips, let me first start off by saying that I'm not going to tell you to give away all of your belongings and force you to pretend to be happy with merely the clothes on your back. Rest assured, I still enjoy my Jeep Wrangler, house with a pool, pretty clothing and the world's most influential water-holding container—my Stanley cup (it seriously still blows my mind the way that the Stanley water cup took over the internet; oh, the power of branding). Anyway, my point is that I still enjoy the material things that matter to me. I believe there's a balance to be found in appreciating what we have while still seeking deeper meaning. In no way am I far enough along on my own spiritual detachment journey to shed all my belongings, move to Eastern Asia, and join a monastery. If and when I get closer to that point, I'm sure I'll write another book on that. Just don't hold your breath because it took me a while to even get to the point I'm currently at, and I'm still a work in progress.

While there are hundreds of books dedicated to Buddhist teachings on topics like detachment, many are so far removed from Western culture that it can be nearly impossible to grasp the concepts, especially if you've never heard them before. The polarity between Eastern and Western cultures is extreme in many ways, and it requires a lot of curiosity, interest, and open-mindedness to embrace a completely new way of thinking and being. I've been very curious in my approach to merge the best of both cultures together, and I've been learning how to infuse many of the beautiful Eastern philosophies into my Western roots. This has required a lot of deep thought, reflection, and some creativity to figure out how to merge the best of both worlds into one. So far, I feel like I'm on the right track.

Eastern cultures are often characterized by a strong connection with nature, spirituality, and ethical values. My personal research indicates that these cultures tend to emphasize wellness, cohesion, peace, tranquillity, connection, and purpose. Additionally, they are deeply rooted in ancestral practices that have stood the test of time, reflecting a holistic approach to life that prioritizes community and harmony with the environment. Western culture, in contrast, often emphasizes personal achievement, independence, financial gain, status, and materialism. In our Western culture there can be a tendency to sideline traditional teachings and values in favour of new technologies and progressive developments. Without Western culture, I don't think we'd be as advanced as a species. However, in the absence of Eastern culture, we aren't able to fully appreciate those convenient advancements without the consequences of overindulgence and inharmonious balance.

Basically, we need to learn how to appreciate all the new tools, technologies, medical advancements, and so on without losing our humanity in the process. This chapter shares my experiences in applying these teachings in a practical, straightforward way—making them easy for you to understand and even easier to incorporate into your own life. I'm just your average Canadian girl trying to infuse meaning, purpose, and fulfilment into my life while sharing my wake-up-and-smell-the-coffee moments with you so that you can learn to live more intentionally, too. I'll share my method for enjoying material things without tying my identity to them, emotionally attaching to them, holding onto them as trophies, letting them inflate my ego, or allowing them to define my self-worth.

To achieve this, embracing detachment is key. It's not about getting rid of all our belongings and pretending not to enjoy material things entirely—insert deep breath and sigh of relief here. Rather, it's about deciphering which things truly matter to us and which we can happily live without. Accepting that we do not need the best of everything and learning to create healthy boundaries with our material possessions is essential. By doing this, we can own our belongings without letting them own us. Ultimately, it's about learning to release the desire and pressure to keep up with the Joneses. Embracing this journey brings a profound sense of freedom, allowing us to live with intention and authenticity.

I want you to start by thinking about some of your most valuable possessions. What are they? Maybe your car, your home, a collector's item, a sports jersey, a designer purse, a pair of shoes, jewellery, or a piece of clothing—it could be anything that you love. The key word here is love. That's where the problem of attachment lies. Detachment happens when we learn how to stop *loving* our things. It's the feeling of love that has to go. That's why the saying goes: love people, use things, because love and emotional expressions should be reserved for connections and relationships. Research shows that individuals who prioritize relationships over material possessions experience greater happiness and life satisfaction. In many Eastern philosophies, detachment from materialism is seen as a path to spiritual growth and deeper connections.

We've been influenced by marketing and advertising companies to believe the products that we're being sold should make us feel a certain way emotionally. They condition us to believe that if we don't own those products, we should feel worse off because of it. Consider this: how often have you purchased something with the hope that it would fill an emotional void or elevate your status? Marketing and advertising companies understand human psychology well, and they're not afraid to exploit it to their advantage if it means making a sale. You might also have other feelings surrounding your most coveted belongings, such as admiration or pride, that must also be addressed. We need to remove these emotional attachments altogether and accept our things for exactly what they are—things, stuff, objects, belongings, articles, tools, possessions... you get the point. By doing so, we can reclaim our emotional well-being and focus on what truly enriches our lives: meaningful connections with others.

The reason we develop emotions and cling to physical items is that doing so makes us feel more permanent—even though, deep down, we know we're only here temporarily. Surrounding ourselves with objects gives us a sense of lasting presence in a world where everything, including us, is destined to fade. This attachment can provide a sense of identity and security, especially in a fast-paced world where everything seems transient. This is an illusion. In fact, the actual act of owning anything at all is one of the greatest illusions of all time. We get a false sense of safety and security from owning land or owning our homes when really, everything we think we own is just on loan until we die. There is nothing in the world that we actually own. Society wants us to believe in the "ownership of things" so that we continue to spend money on them and keep the economy going, but it's all smoke and mirrors. This perpetual cycle of consumption can lead to feelings of inadequacy and dissatisfaction, as we chase after the next possession that promises happiness, only to find that true fulfilment lies beyond material ownership. From now on, I want you to think of everything that you "own" as a rental that you're borrowing for your short time here on Earth. When you pass away, your house, car, purse, shoes, phone, jewellery, clothing, tools, and everything else will be passed on for someone else to borrow. Then, when they die, it will be passed on to someone else, and so on until the objects become worn down and are no longer functional. Consciously, as humans, we don't like to acknowledge just how impermanent we are because it scares us. One might say that it scares us to death—a little dark humour to lighten up this part.

The reality is that we are all going to die, and when we do, all of our belongings will be left here in the physical world without us. A simple stroll through an antique store brings this truth to light, revealing items that were once cherished by those who have since passed away. Each weathered trinket and faded photograph holds a whisper of the past that has since surrendered to the relentless passage of time. Possessions are all that remain, steeped in memories, while their owners have long since died. I encourage you to wander through those old antique shops, where time stands still among the dusty shelves. As you browse the aisles, let the tips of your fingers subtly graze the worn leather covers of aged books, the delicate curves of vintage sewing machines, and the polished surfaces of timeworn typewriters. Imagine the lives that these objects once touched—the laughter shared over a well-loved dining table or the secrets typed out on a forgotten desk. Feel the weight of history in the air, a bittersweet reminder of the fleeting nature of existence. As you stroll, imagine the false sense of security and artificial love these objects once brought to their previous owners. Picture their hands using or touching their belongings for the very last time. The previous owners of these objects likely experienced the same kind of superficial love that you and I have felt for our own possessions. Now, I invite you to picture your most cherished belongings finding their way here one day, too. Envision them resting on a weathered shelf, nestled among the forgotten treasures of another life, their vibrant colours fading into the muted tones of time. A bright orange price tag clings to the bottom, a stark reminder of their past value, now diminished by the inevitability of time. This is the destiny that all of our cherished belongings face—awaiting for the next stranger to pass by and trace their fingers over the thin veil of forgotten memories.

I know it can feel jarring to accept that one day our belongings will no longer belong to us, but it is the reality. It's why our material things are all that will remain long after we're gone. If we can learn to emotionally detach ourselves from our belongings before death forces us to do it involuntarily, we will be able to experience true freedom in this physical world and fully focus our attention on what really matters—loving people and using things.

Imagine a world where we cherish moments over objects, where laughter shared with friends around a dinner table holds more value than the aesthetic decoration of the room itself. By shifting our focus away from material items and embracing the principles of the science of happiness discussed in Chapter Three, we open ourselves to a deeper, richer, and more elevated human experience. This newfound perspective allows us to feel truly free, using our material possessions as tools to enhance our lives while reserving our emotions for love and connection.

Detachment happens when we learn to be able to still enjoy material things without feeling an emotional attachment to them. For example, think of your most favourite possessions—shoes, handbags, equipment, vehicles, devices. Now, consider how it would make you feel to not have them. For most people, this will drum up all kinds of emotions: anger, sadness, fear, unhappiness, unworthiness, etc. Detachment is the process of removing these emotions that we feel toward our material things in a way that allows us to genuinely (not resentfully) stop feeling them. Basically, you'll know that you've fully detached yourself from a material item when it wouldn't matter to you whether you owned it or not.

I'll give you an example. If not having your coveted Louis Vuitton purse anymore would make you extremely unhappy and upset, then you are emotionally attached to it. By being emotionally attached to a physical object, you set yourself up for inevitable disappointment. After all, you could lose the purse, it could become damaged, or someone could steal it. How would you feel then? Chances are, you'd be very upset with any of those situations. These are the real possibilities that come along with "owning" physical items. Now, if any of those situations happened to someone who had been practicing detachment, they would just think, "Oh well, it was only a purse..." and move on with their day. A person practicing detachment might appreciate the purse for its functionality and design, but their happiness wouldn't hinge on its possession. Maybe they would buy another one; maybe they wouldn't, but either way, they wouldn't feel an emotional attachment to the object, regardless of what happened to it. This emotional attachment is precisely what marketing companies capitalize on. They know that we are emotional beings, and they skillfully exploit this fact to influence our purchasing decisions. Unless we intentionally learn to redirect our emotions to things that genuinely matter—such as meaningful relationships, personal growth, and enriching experiences—our feelings will run rampant in all directions, leaking into almost every area of our lives. For example, if you're into designer brands, you likely chose to buy the designer purse over a less expensive, similarly high-quality unbranded one because of how it made you feel emotionally. It likely made you feel special, important, beautiful, desirable, fashionable, or prestigious. High-end luxury brands often target our emotions rather than our practical needs, leading us to make purchases that don't serve our true well-being (regardless of the story you concoct to tell your spouse). These items often carry the allure of status and identity rather than offering genuine functionality. Ultimately, recognizing this manipulation can empower us to make more intentional choices about where we invest our time, energy, and resources. It is especially hard to detach from these luxury items due to the emotional ties we form with them, which can create a sense of loss or identity crisis when we consider letting go. You'll first need to unpack the emotional reasons why you chose to purchase them in the first place. Purchasing luxury items can often be a way of covering up unresolved baggage, emotional issues, and insecurities in an attempt to make yourself feel more worthy, desirable, important, or to appear wealthy to others. This desire for external validation can lead to a cycle of dependency on material possessions, where the temporary boost in self-esteem fades, leaving us searching for the next purchase to fill the void. I know it can be hard to hear, but sometimes your Louis Vuitton purse is a bat signal for a greater emotional issue that needs tending to. Perhaps it's time for you and Louis to have a heart-to-heart. Recognizing these emotional attachments is a crucial step toward detachment. If you have no emotions bubbling to the surface at the thought of parting ways with your items then you are that much closer to achieving it. It's important to learn how to start appreciating things for the real purpose they provide, rather than the emotions they evoke. A purse, for example, obviously holds a purpose: to carry your belongings when you're out and about. It is absolutely possible to still enjoy and appreciate the purse for the function it serves. You can appreciate its functionality and admire its aesthetic, while simultaneously learning to be emotionally fine if you didn't have it. Much like luxury items, family heirlooms and trinkets passed down through generations can hold a similar emotional significance. Regardless of their importance or value, these items are still physical objects, and learning to detach from them is equally important.

What items do you have in your life right now that you feel you'd never be able to part ways with? Start by identifying those things and work with yourself until you can honestly say that you no longer feel any emotional attachments to them. Doing a visualization practice has helped me slowly become detached from sentimental objects in my own life. I close my eyes and envision someone else discovering my most cherished possessions long after I'm gone. I picture them unearthing each item, finding joy and utility in what I once held dear. With every visualization, I feel my attachment loosening its grip, transforming into a sense of liberation. Instead of dwelling on the emptiness that might come from letting go, I shift my focus to the value and functionality these items will bring to their new owner's life. Bonus points if you can physically part ways with some of these things right now by donating or giving them to someone who would find them useful. It will be one less thing you have to practice detaching from. You'll be physically creating detachment by intentionally removing it from your life and witnessing your life carry on without it. It'll only be a matter of time before you likely forget you ever even owned it.

My very first experience with detachment came shortly after returning home from being sick in the hospital, as I shared in Chapter One. The day that I came home, I was flooded with gratitude instantly as I walked through my front door. Being able to leave the sterile white walls, the potent scent of hospital-grade sanitizers, and the sound of constant humming from hospital equipment felt like a breath of fresh air. Returning to my vibrant lime-green living room—surrounded by photographs I'd taken during my world travels and the soothing scent of diffused berg-amot—overwhelmed my senses with a newfound appreci-ation of being home. In that moment, I realized how much I had taken for granted. My home had been my sanctuary, and as an introvert, it's where I enjoyed spending most of my time. I had previously invested a lot of time and money into renovating it and adding amenities to make my home feel like the ultimate retreat from the outside world. There's a room upstairs that I turned into a studio and dedicated to my art and photography; a room that I transformed into an at-home gym; a full-size indoor swimming pool in the basement; a hot tub overlooking the nature ravine in the backyard; a luxurious primary bedroom with an ensuite bathroom that has a double-sided fireplace; and a wellness shed in the backyard equipped with an infrared sauna and cold plunge tub. If heaven was a place on earth, this was it for me. I loved it, and the more money I invested into customizing it and making it my own, the more attached I became to it. Unfortunately, my gratitude for returning home from the hospital to my self-made paradise was short-lived, as it quickly dissolved into fear when a terrifying thought crossed my mind. Some people who end up in the hospital never get to experience this feeling of coming home again because they don't get to return home at all. Some people who go to the hospital end up dying in the hospital. They never get to experience the feeling of walking through their own front door ever again. This realization left me feeling exposed and vulnerable as I slowly began to come to terms with the truth that I didn't truly own any of this at all. As these thoughts weighed heavily on me, it became clear that there will always be a last time for everything, including walking down my stairs and out my own front door for the very last time.

And then what? I thought to myself. If I died in the hospital, someone else would eventually buy and live in my home. I pictured another family living in my space, sleeping in my bed, brushing their teeth in my sink, making pancakes in my kitchen, and hosting Christmas dinner in my house. My house! This thought did not sit well with me, and yet I could not, for the life of me, stop pondering it. It consumed my mind for several months, as I could not make peace with this idea. It didn't take long for this thought to start spiralling, which led me to also think about everything else that I owned inside the house. The fact that someone else would gain access to all the rest of my belongings too—my paintings, my journals, my favourite pair of leopard-print heels, my wedding dress, my favourite coffee mugs, my couch, my bed, and my car made me squirm. Even as I write this, I don't know how to do my words justice in explaining just how horrendous I felt at the thought of sur-rendering my home and all of my belongings to someone else. Consequently, I had nightmares and very depressive thoughts for several months. I couldn't stop thinking about it, and I desperately wanted to revert back to my pre-hos-pital self, where my naivety kept me safe and sane from such intrusive thoughts. I knew that I needed to figure this out so that I could stop torturing myself, so I went ahead and started researching my feelings in hopes of finding an answer as to what I should do about it. That's when I stumbled upon the concept of detachment. I spent a great deal of time reading and researching it until I felt confident enough to try implementing it. Slowly, I began to under-stand the concept, but I wasn't sure exactly how to put it into practice. I wanted to start with the object that felt the most valuable to me—the one that made me feel all kinds of intensely attached emotions: comfort, happiness, safety, joy, peace, pride, and the very thing that got me thinking about this entire concept in the first place—my home. I thought of all the different ways I could detach myself from my emotional attachment to it. I considered moving, but I quickly realized that by replacing one object with another, I wouldn't alleviate the underlying attachment that I felt. If I moved, I would just end up moving into another home that I'd have to learn how to detach myself from. I was trying to get creative in my approach to detaching myself from my home while still learning how to appreciate and enjoy it for the comfort and shelter it provided my physical body. Eventually, it dawned on me and I remembered the part of the science of happiness equation that talked about how adding people to experiences creates meaning, purpose, and happiness. This gave me an idea for an experiment: what if I periodically traded my home with other people and shared my little piece of paradise with them? They could stay at my home, and I would stay at theirs. I loved travelling and exploring, and anytime my husband and I went away, our home just sat empty, unused, and vacant. This idea reminded me of the movie *The Holiday*, one of my favourite movies of all time. I thought that maybe by providing other people access to my home and allowing them to stay there for short periods of time to enjoy all the peace and tranquillity that it provided, I would become less attached to the idea that my home was mine and more open to other people enjoying it too. It seemed a little cringey at first, and if I'm being completely honest, it took a little while for me to warm up to the idea that strangers would be sleeping (among doing other things) in my bed. However, the more I thought about it and realized that anytime I stayed at an Airbnb or hotel room, I was sleeping (among doing other things) in someone else's bed that many strangers had previously slept in before. I understood it really wasn't that different or strange after all. We're all just humans, and if I was willing to sleep in hotels or Airbnbs with beds that had been slept in by many people before me, then why should it bother me to have other humans in my bed? All you need to get is some separate bedding, extra pillows, and a bottle of bleach. Next, I had to get over the fear of all the worst-case scenarios—people trashing my place, breaking things, partying irresponsibly, leaving it a disaster, etc. It's funny how our minds go straight to the worst-case scenarios and not the best-case ones (being human is fucking strange sometimes, you guys). Our brains are always in survival mode, eager to point out the worst-case possibilities without evaluating the probability of them actually happening. It's the same reason people are afraid to swim in the ocean for fear of a shark bite, even though, statistically, it's very unlikely. The more we recognize the tricks our minds play, the better we are at intervening and interrupting those autopilot, fear-mongering thought patterns. I had to accept that if I was going to attempt detaching from my home, this would be a pretty radical way to test the concept.

I began researching how to share or trade my home with others. Lo and behold, I stumbled upon a website that had been facilitating home swapping for over twenty years. On this website, you can trade homes with people from all over the world for free. There is a nominal annual fee to be part of the exchange community, along with a verification process, but other than that, it's as simple as it sounds. I couldn't believe this existed without me knowing about it all this time. Then again, even if I had discovered it years earlier, I wouldn't have been open to the idea back then. What really struck me as ironic, though, was that this very platform had already appeared in one of my favourite Christmas movies—*The Holiday*. Cameron Diaz and Kate Winslet used this exact site to swap their homes in the film. I can't tell you how many times I've watched that movie (every year around Christmas for what seems like forever) and never once noticed the website. What are the odds? The fact that this site had been around for years with a solid reputation gave me the reassurance I needed to sign up and participate.

Fast forward to the present moment as I'm writing this book, and I've been using this site for almost two years now, trading my home with over a dozen different people worldwide. I can confidently say that sharing my home has not only helped me learn to detach from it, but has also taught me a new dimension of joy, brought on by others' expressions of gratitude and happiness when they enjoy and relax in my home. There's actually a word that best describes this feeling that I learned about in Elizabeth Gilbert's book *Big Magic* called *Freudenfreude*, a German word defined as "finding pleasure in another person's good fortune or happiness." Could there be a more beautiful word to embrace and live by? I don't think so. I definitely feel immense and immeasurable joy by sharing my material things with others who appreciate them. It actually brings me a much greater sense of happiness to share my things than it does to simply own them and keep them all to myself. There's something magical that happens when we share our things or open our homes to others that's difficult to explain until you try it for yourself. Every time I read a thank-you card thoughtfully left behind by a guest, my heart melts hearing about how great of a time they had enjoying our home with their families. Knowing that I contributed to their memory-making is as meaningful as it gets. After realizing that everyone in this online exchange community is a homeowner with similar fears and reservations, it doesn't take long to establish trust in each other as you swap homes.

I'd like to end this chapter with a very powerful true story of the impermanence of time that segues into my next chapter of living in the present moment. Back when I first found out about exchanging homes, I'd joined some Facebook groups dedicated to helping people navigate questions, concerns, offering advice and tips on how home exchanging works. This whole concept was foreign to me, and I was extremely nervous and skeptical about trading homes with strangers. As you can imagine, I had a lot of questions. I started asking my questions and concerns in the groups as they came to mind. One woman, in particular, consistently stood out for her eagerness to help, always providing thoughtful and thorough answers to all my inquiries. Her name was Lena, and I would always see Lena's name pop up as the very first comment on any of my posts. She was so consistent and diligent in her responses, and she was the first person to really make me feel comfortable and confident in my decision to add my home to the site. I was so grateful to have connected with someone who offered honest and authentic feedback and who took the time to chat with me on several occasions. Being new to the site, I didn't have any reviews and, as a result, was having a difficult time finding people who would exchange with me. It was one of those things that in order to get reviews, I needed to stay somewhere, but in order to stay somewhere, I needed to have reviews. Lena graciously proposed that we do an exchange together. She offered me the chance to stay in her cozy cottage in North Carolina, and she was equally thrilled about the prospect of visiting my place in Canada. I couldn't contain my excitement as I prepared to officially book my first exchange and see how the experience unfolded. We planned our home exchange a few months in advance for the fall. The idea of swapping homes is not the only exciting part, but it also opens the door to meeting incredible people from all around the world—this is truly the highlight for me. We connected on social media, and during one memorable conversation, she opened up sharing her enthusiasm about officially retiring next year after a fulfilling career as a registered nurse. She was eager to finally have the time and freedom to travel whenever and wherever she wanted. She shared details about a few pre-planned trips that were on the horizon. I could sense her zest for life and passion for travel, as if her high vibrational energy was being transmitted right through my computer screen. Though we hadn't met in person, I couldn't help but be ecstatic on her behalf about her upcoming retirement and future freedom. It all sounded like a dream come true.

A few months passed, and as our exchange date approached, Lena sent me a message one evening. She regrettably informed me that she needed to cancel our plans due to medical reasons, which would prevent her from travelling. Being as this was supposed to be my first exchange, truthfully, I didn't know what to make of it. She'd always been so eager and excited, and this time it felt abrupt and short. I wasn't sure why she didn't suggest rescheduling for a later date instead of straight-up cancelling. Many thoughts crossed my mind. I wondered if maybe after getting to know me, she didn't trust me enough to stay at her house. Perhaps I'd posted something on social media that she took offense to, or maybe she just didn't want to come to my house and found somewhere better to visit... I didn't know. Naturally, I was racking my brain for all the things I might have been at fault for. Disappointed and skeptical of the reason for the cancellation, I kept my response short and wished her a quick recovery back to health. There wasn't much communication after that, and I noticed that her name stopped popping up in the comments of the group chats, offering her helpful advice. I remember hoping that she was okay.

The date we had originally planned to exchange had come and gone, and about a week after we were supposed to exchange homes, I came across a post on Facebook... It was Lena's obituary. She had just passed away from an aggressive form of cancer. I was stunned and in shock. I was just talking to her a few months earlier about her future hopes and dreams. How could this have happened so quickly? It brings tears to my eyes as I write this because all I can think about is the travel plans she was making and how excited she was to finally retire and seize the opportunity to do exactly what she'd always wanted. She was unknowingly unaware that her time on earth was coming to an abrupt and premature end before she'd get to experience any of that. I was overwhelmed with sadness. This tragic turn of events serves as a powerful reminder of life's unpredictable nature and the urgency of pursuing our dreams. It compels us to reflect on the importance of living authentically and with intention, seizing each moment with the understanding that tomorrow is never guaranteed. In honouring Lena's memory, we must embrace our own aspirations and passions, ensuring that we don't postpone the experiences that bring us joy and fulfillment, for they are the threads that weave the fabric of a meaningful life.

This chapter was a hard one to write and I know it's been a difficult one to read. It's been an emotional journey to come to terms with my own impermanence and mortality, but it's through learning about detachment and the concept of loving people and using things that we can truly appreciate every single moment and align our lives authentically. The price we pay for the experience of life is death. Lena taught me that while we can plan for the future, the future might not be in our plans.

Life doesn't wait for our retirement;

It doesn't wait for us to take our next vacation.

It quite literally doesn't wait for anything.

It's here, and then it isn't.

We're here, and then we're gone.

We're alive, and then we're dead.

Life won't wait, and neither should we—

It's time to live fully, fiercely, and free.

Chapter Eight
WELCOME TO THE PRESENT

Have you ever talked to someone who was physically present but mentally somewhere else entirely?

Or perhaps you've been the one lost in your thoughts while someone spoke to you?

Have you ever driven home, only to arrive without a clue of how you got there because you were totally zoned out?

Or been in class, at a conference, or in a lecture, daydreaming or thinking about everything you needed to do once you got home?

Perhaps you can relate to reading a book and realizing midway through the chapter that you have no idea what you just read, ending up having to re-read it.

Have you ever spent time with someone glued to their phone, constantly checking it during your visit?

Or maybe you've been the one distracted by your device, flinching at every notification that goes off...

Numerous distractions prevent us from being fully present in our daily lives and tasks at hand. Despite the abundance of books, podcasts, blogs, and other content highlighting the importance of the present moment, we often let it all flow in one ear and out the other. This topic is frequently discussed, yet it remains largely underutilized and misunderstood. Unless we actively practice the skill of being present, we never will be. Our minds are naturally inclined to wander—dwelling on the past and anxiously anticipating the future. We spend very little time consciously and intentionally living in the present moment. This is very concerning because the only moment that ever exists is the present moment. The past and future are not real. To escape this cycle, understand that genuine happiness, peace, and freedom are found in the practice of living in the present moment. It begins with recognizing and valuing the small moments that shape the present. Life truly comes alive when you become mindful of the significance of the present moment.

I had no idea how little time I spent truly living in the present moment. It wasn't until I experienced what it meant to be present that I realized just how life-changing it could be. Living in the present means tuning into all of your senses and focusing solely on what you're currently doing, no matter how significant or routine the task may seem. Whether you're washing dishes, folding laundry, reading a book, cleaning the house, working, or—my personal favourite—enjoying a cup of coffee, the key is to be fully engaged, aware, conscious, and present in whatever you're doing.

Here's an example. Let's say you're sitting on the couch enjoying your morning coffee, being in the present moment means focusing solely on that—sitting on the couch and savouring your coffee. Tune into how you feel and what you're experiencing in that exact moment. How does the coffee taste? How does the warm cup feel against the palms of your hands? Take a deep inhale and breathe in the aromatic scent of the coffee as the steam disintegrates into the air. How does it smell? Notice how your body feels at that moment. Is it relaxed and well-rested from a good night's sleep, or are you feeling sore and achy from yesterday's workout? Engaging as many of our five senses (taste, touch, smell, sight, and sound) as possible helps to keep us in the present moment at any given time. Before I learned how to enjoy the moment and be present, I would mindlessly sip my coffee while scrolling through social media on my phone as I pondered what I should make for breakfast and what I was going to do for the duration of the day. Before I knew it, my coffee was gone, and I had no recollection of even drinking it. In both situations, I'm doing the exact same thing—enjoying my morning coffee. However, in the first example, I'm actively being present in what I'm doing, and in the second example, I'm allowing my mind to wander into the future. Embracing the present moment transforms mundane activities into rich experiences, allowing us to fully appreciate the simple joys of life.

There are indeed moments when it's important to plan for the future and reflect on the past. We often need to set goals, organize events, book vacations, or schedule appointments. Likewise, it's important to take moments to reflect, learn from our mistakes, acknowledge our progress, and appreciate those who have influenced our lives. The problem is that we've learned to make past and future thinking the predominant way of living while paying little to no attention to living in the present moment. We need to substantially reverse this. While planning and reflection are valuable, we must learn to shift our focus back to the present moment to truly engage with and appreciate our lives.

When we practice being fully present and consciously aware of our actions 90% of the time, dedicating just 5% to planning for the future and another 5% to reflecting on the past, we can significantly enhance our overall happiness. To achieve this, we need to start practicing bringing our minds back to the present moment every time we notice it wandering into future or past thinking. It's all about retraining our minds. The more we train ourselves to notice when our minds start to wander and bring our focus back to the present moment, the less our minds will wander over time. Eventually, we won't have to focus so hard on monitoring and intercepting our thoughts. As with any new habit, it will feel challenging at first, but I promise it gets easier over time. I can attest that when I first learned to be more present in my life, it felt very foreign. I was shocked when I realized just how little time I had been spending in the present. As I became more mindful and practiced being present, my body and mind began to crave living in the present moment even more. Once you gain momentum and experience the sense of aliveness it brings, you'll no longer allow your mind to drift aimlessly into past or future thoughts.

The reason we need to learn how to start living in the present moment is that it is the only moment that truly exists. If you think about it logically, we aren't guaranteed to wake up tomorrow. Therefore, any future plans that we spent all day yesterday conjuring up for today could hypothetically never happen. When we do this, we end up wasting the present moment by distracting ourselves with over-planning and worrying about future things that may never occur. Even if the things you were pre-planning for do end up happening, they still rob you of the present moment. The best thing that you can do when making future plans is to make them, add them to your calendar, and never think about them again until you're in the present moment doing them. You have no idea how much anxiety and stress you will rid yourself of by learning to live like this on a regular basis. Consider how much time you've spent over the years worrying about future plans—what to wear, who will be there, or what the weather might be like. The issue isn't in making the plans themselves; that takes just a few minutes. It's the time we waste afterward, allowing those worries to distract us from the present moment. That's where we need to focus our attention. We often end up sacrificing hours worrying, stressing, and overthinking about upcoming plans—time that would be better spent fully enjoying the present moment.

Our present moments are all we truly have, so it's essential to cherish them—they're the only true measure of time we're guaranteed. It's disheartening to recognize how easily we sacrifice these moments for thoughts of a past or future that don't even exist in reality. We all understand, in theory, that time is our most valuable asset, yet we often fail to truly value it or treat it with the respect it deserves. We tend to be very careful and intentional with resources like money, so why aren't we equally (if not more) cautious

and intentional about not wasting our most precious asset—time?

In terms of past tense thinking, it's clear that we've already experienced our past and cannot return to relive those moments. Therefore, the past is essentially non-existent in the same way the future is non-existent. Though our past experiences feel real to us, they're no longer part of our current reality—they exist only as memories. When we hold onto these moments, we're choosing to live in a time that has already passed, allowing shadows of what was to intrude on what *is*. The more we let go of the past, the more space we create to fully engage with our present, building a life that honours each moment we're actually living in.

When we commit to living in the present, a remarkable transformation occurs, unlocking a world of clarity, peace, and a deeper connection to our everyday experiences. Our senses get heightened and relationships become deeper. We learn to be grateful for the simple things in our lives, and most importantly, we start to feel like time slows down in a way that makes us feel like we're getting the most out of it. You'll notice that when you become fully present and engage all of your senses in each moment, time actually feels like it's moving much slower, thus giving you the perception that you have more of it. Don't we all want to feel like we have more time? In a world where everyone is constantly bitching and complaining that they don't have enough time to do the things they say they want to do, can you imagine what a gift it would be to actually feel like you have more of it? That's what living in the present moment does—it slows things down and makes you feel like you have more time. Have you ever recalled a memory and felt like it had just happened yesterday when, in fact, it happened three years ago? That's what happens when you're not consciously living in the present moment. It actually makes you feel like life is passing by without you. Not being present feels like you're trapped in a scene from a movie, standing on a sidewalk as a chaotic whirlwind rushes past you—people, cars, and moments blurring together. By contrast, slowing down and being present with whatever you're currently doing allows each day to feel fully experienced and enjoyed to its maximum capacity. You'll find that instead of feeling like things are moving too fast, your sense of time will become more practical, and it will start to have the opposite effect. You'll look back on something that happened three years ago, and it will feel like it could have been six years ago because you've been so present in everything that you do. When we are present, time feels like it moves much slower because we aren't distracted by future or past thoughts, and we get to engage all of our senses in the enjoyment of whatever it is that we're doing. To illustrate this, think about being on a treadmill (or a dreadmill, as I like to call it) and imagine focusing only on the present moment while you're on it. You're walking or running, your feet are moving swiftly, your arms are propelling you forward, and you feel the sweat trickling down your forehead. With every stride that your foot hits the rubbery belt, you hear an annoying squeaky sound. How slow does time feel when you're focused on the present moment the entire time that you're on that treadmill? It's painfully slow. There's a reason why we listen to music or watch a video on our phones to distract us from the present moment when on a treadmill; it makes time feel like it's moving faster.

Life is no different. The more distractions we engage in, the faster it goes. Conversely, the more we focus on what we are doing, the slower time feels. There are certainly times when listening to music or watching videos makes sense to help time pass more quickly—like on the treadmill, during workouts, on flights, in hospitals, or when we're feeling unwell—moments that are naturally unenjoyable to be fully present for. However, the real issue arises when we live our lives in a relentless state of distraction, resulting in a hollow existence that rushes by in a blur, leaving us with nothing but a nagging sense of unfulfilment.

The best resource that I can recommend regarding learning all about the present moment and how to consciously live in it is called *The Power of Now* by Eckhart Tolle. I highly recommend reading it and can pretty much guarantee that you'll need to read it more than once in order to understand it thoroughly. To this day, it's a book that I continuously re-read when I need a refresher.

Living in the present moment can significantly reduce stress, depression, and anxiety. Most of the time, it's not our current situations that create these negative feelings but rather our thoughts about the past and future that lead to stress, worry, and sadness. How is it possible to be drinking your morning cup of coffee in the comfort and safety of your own home while feeling depressed or anxious from simply doing that? Surely, it's not the literal action of you drinking the coffee on the couch that is making you feel depressed or anxious. It's whatever thoughts you're having that are mentally taking you out of that current moment that are creating feelings of stress, depression, and anxiety. If you solely focused on the enjoyment of drinking your coffee on the couch, you would feel totally content and at ease. Since our thoughts shape our feelings, it's essential to be mindful of what we allow ourselves to think about. If you find yourself sipping your coffee while your mind drifts to past moments—like yesterday's meeting with your boss, who gave you a negative performance review—those negative thoughts can spiral into feelings of distress, completely hijacking the peace and serenity of that present moment. I like to call this polluting your present moment. You're creating your own personal "present moment pollution" that doesn't need to be there. When reflecting on that moment with your boss, it's natural to feel upset. However, it's essential to avoid continuously reliving past experiences that can taint your current moments—those that could otherwise be enjoyable—by letting your mind rewind and replay negative memories. Instead, embrace your feelings as they arise, acknowledge them, and decide what you will do differently to ensure better outcomes in the future. Once you've addressed them, let them go and move forward.

There are countless ways that past thinking and future thinking show up in our lives. I'm going to list a few of the most common ones below, along with the reasons why we need to stop doing them and how you can bring yourself back to the present moment when they arise:

Ways That Future Thinking Shows Up in Our Lives:

1. Looking forward to an upcoming vacation, event, concert, or anything else exciting.

2. Feeling anxious about a speech, presentation, or attending a networking event.

3. Worrying about what the weather will be like next month when you have to drive five hours out of town for something important.

4. Setting future goals of any kind—career, fitness, health, financial, etc.

5. Overthinking what to wear to an important event, like a job interview or a first date.

6. Daydreaming about future accomplishments or milestones.

Why We Need to Significantly Limit Future Thinking:

Anything that we anticipate happening in the future is uncertain, meaning that it may or may not happen. Why on earth would we waste so much of our time in the present moment thinking about, anticipating, worrying, or getting excited about something that may or may not happen in the future? It just doesn't seem like a good use of time. There is simply no way of knowing what the future will hold because we may or may not still be alive at the time of the anticipated event. Remember, we aren't invincible, and we will all die one day. We aren't guaranteed the future, and we need to stop acting like we are. Daydreaming and planning for the future are distracting us from enjoying our lives in the only moment we have—the present moment. Don't fool yourself into thinking that positive future thoughts, like goal-setting, anticipating a vacation, or fantasizing about future successes, are exceptions to this rule. Even these seemingly uplifting thoughts can sabotage our ability to find joy in the present moment.

How to Bring Yourself Back to the Present Moment When Future Thoughts Arise:

It's important to be aware that we aren't trying to eliminate these thoughts completely; it would be pretty much impossible to do that. Be patient and kind with yourself, allowing the thoughts to come while swiftly sending them on their way. When it comes to goals, instead of fantasizing about the end result and how happy you'll be once you achieve those goals, it's more productive to decide what you can do today, in the present moment, that will help get you closer to them. There's a lot of talk in the self-development world about how we need to enjoy the journey toward our goals because if we don't focus on enjoying the journey, then, once the goal comes and goes, we'll realize just how quickly the sense of accomplishment dissipates. The reason we have to learn to enjoy the journey toward the goal is that the journey is where we spend the majority of our time prior to achieving the goal. Think about any goal you've ever achieved. How long did you spend working toward the goal vs. how long did you spend in the moment that you actually achieved it? Most of our time is spent on the journey toward achieving the goal. Make sure that you are present throughout the process and that you make it as exciting and enjoyable as you anticipate the achievement to be. When people work really hard to achieve a goal without enjoying the journey, they typically end up very depressed afterward. You hear it all the time with athletes: they win a gold medal and then end up depressed shortly after the dopamine high of the accomplishment wears off because they were over-glorifying the end goal and under-appreciating the journey of working toward it. During their pursuit of the goal, they became so distracted by the allure of the achievement that they convinced themselves that the goal itself would magically provide them with a sense of accomplishment. They didn't recognize that the true value lies in the growth, lessons, and experiences gained along the way. The journey is filled with moments of discovery, resilience, and connection, which are essential for cultivating a deep sense of fulfilment. By shifting our focus from merely the outcome to the richness of the process, we create a more sustainable source of joy and satisfaction that enhances our overall well-being.

In terms of being excited for a future event (such as a vacation, concert, etc.), allow yourself to enjoy that excitement for exactly one minute when the thought arises, then redirect your attention back to the present moment. Don't let the anticipatory excitement rob you of the joy and gift of what you're doing right now—because if you let it, it will. Sure, the laundry you're folding might seem less appealing than the cruise you'll be boarding in six months. But remember, being alive in the moment you're in, even while folding laundry, is far more precious than the fact that you could die tomorrow and never get the opportunity to board that cruise. Also, when we place excessive excitement and emphasis on future events, like a vacation, we often experience a significant letdown once the event is over. When you spend each day looking forward to a future event, you're subconsciously hyping it up. When that event comes and goes, you're back in the present moment without anything to anticipate, often leaving you feeling lost, wondering, "Now what?" This is why people get stuck in a loop of constantly needing something to look forward to—and why they often find themselves planning their next vacation on the first day back to work. It may seem harmless to let yourself daydream about future events, but all it's really doing is robbing you of the present moment. By looking forward to things in the future, you're simultaneously devaluing the only moment that exists: right now. You can't be excited about a future event while fully embracing the present moment; you're either doing one or the other.

This will resonate with anyone who looks forward to their two-week vacation all year, only to feel a deep sense of sadness when they return to reality. There are fifty-two weeks in a year. Learning to enjoy and appreciate the other fifty, instead of being miserable while waiting for those two weeks of vacation, is essential. The solution is to craft your daily reality to reflect a life that you actually look forward to returning to after enjoying a beautiful vacation. Think about what makes vacations so special to you: the freedom, relaxation, new experiences, or quality time. How can you bring elements of these into your daily life? It's important to take inventory of everything in your routine that you don't look forward to returning to and either get rid of it or change it. We are in full control of our lives and how we choose to show up and participate. Personally, I can genuinely say that I love being home in my everyday routine just as much as I love travelling, taking a vacation, going to a concert, or attending an event because I've intentionally created a daily routine that makes me feel fantastic—mentally, physically, spiritually, and emotionally.

Ways That Past Thinking Shows Up in Our Lives:

1. Ruminating about what someone thought of you after they met you.

2. Worrying about whether you said the right thing and replaying the entire conversation in your head over and over again.

3. Thinking about all the things you would have said or done differently in any given situation.

4. Dwelling on past mistakes and constantly revisiting errors or decisions you regret, which prevents you from moving forward.

Why We Need to Significantly Limit Past Thinking:

Ruminating, worrying, thinking, and wondering... These are all things that we do when engaged in past thinking. There's no way for us to go back and fix, change, redirect, or redo any of what has already happened. Is there? Have you been able to time travel back to your past and change anything? I don't think so. So then, why do we torture ourselves by reliving past experiences over and over again in our minds? Let that shit go! A significant amount of mental health issues would be resolved if we learned to remain in the present moment 90% of the time.

Imagine the peace and tranquillity you could experience by letting go of past and future thoughts. The main issue with both past and future thinking is that the mind doesn't distinguish between reality and imagination. Therefore, it triggers the same physical reactions throughout the body as if those events were actually happening. Our minds often gravitate toward negative past events and anxiety-inducing future scenarios, which activate our cortisol and stress responses, even when we are not in real imminent danger. We ignite our own false alarms within our bodies, leading us to live in a chronic state of fight-or-flight. This response was not designed to be activated consistently; the fact that we trigger it non-stop causes various hormonal imbalances (among other negative health effects) within our bodies. Fight-or-flight was meant to be reserved for genuine life-threatening dangers, not simply triggered by our thoughts on a daily basis. If we stop allowing our minds to wander and instead focus on what we are doing in the present moment, we will be significantly less depressed and anxious and much happier overall.

How to Return to the Present Moment When Future Thoughts Arise:

One powerful way to cultivate this present-moment awareness is through meditation. We've all heard about its benefits such as reduced stress, improved focus, and greater emotional resilience. The core purpose of meditation is to quiet the mind and centre our focus on the here and now. The more we can meditate and train our minds to be quiet and still, the more quiet and still our minds will become. In contrast, when we engage in mindless scrolling

on our phones or other distractions, we're negatively training our brains to crave constant stimulation. We're either
training our brains in a positive direction or a negative
one. The more you scroll, the more scattered and less
focused you will become. The more you sit in silence and
meditation, the calmer and more present you will feel. By
incorporating meditation into your routine, even for just a
few minutes each day, you can begin to reclaim your mental
peace and break free from this cycle.

Mindfulness is crucial in this process; it involves recognizing when your thoughts have wandered and gently guiding
yourself back to the present moment. Acknowledge this
happening and refocus your attention on what you're doing right now. It sounds simple because it is. It may feel
overwhelming when you start practicing it, but that's only
because you've spent your entire life without doing so. As
with any new habit or skill, the more you practice, the easier it will become. You will notice your mind wandering a
lot in the beginning, and if you're like me, you'll be shocked
at how often it wanders without you even realizing it at
first. Then, as you begin to recognize it happening and
start to correct it by bringing your attention back to the
present moment, over time, it will wander less and less. It's
important not to strive for perfection in your attempts to
be in the present moment 100% of the time. It is perfectly
healthy for our minds to periodically plan for the future and
reflect on the past. We just want to keep it to an absolute
minimum so that the majority of our time is spent living in
the present moment.

Romanticizing Our Life

As we explore the importance of present-moment awareness and the effects of both past and future thinking, it's
vital to consider practical strategies to maintain our focus.
One approach that has deeply transformed my life—helping me create a daily routine I genuinely look forward to—is
called romanticizing your life. This means slowing down,
being mindful, and fully appreciating the mundane tasks
that shape each day. By finding joy in each moment, this
practice encourages me to stay present. When I began
treating every chore, job, and task as special and meaningful, something shifted, and soon enough, each task genuinely started to feel that way. By intentionally finding joy
in simplicity, it becomes nearly impossible to feel anxious, upset, or disheartened on a regular basis. Practicing
this approach allows your everyday life to evolve into a
higher tier of happiness, a new standard of living, and a
fresh baseline of being. Not only will the fifty weeks of the
year feel significant and fulfilling, but when you do take
a vacation, you'll enjoy it fully and return to regular life
afterward—without the emotional happiness hangover.

Movies do a great job of romanticizing everyday tasks on
the big screen. You see your favourite characters going
out for coffee, strolling through parks, heading to work,
meeting friends, and even grocery shopping—routines that
mirror our own. So why is it that these ordinary scenes
appear so romantic, whimsical, and fun, even when the
main character is just casually picking out tomatoes at
a local market? Personally, there have been many times
I've rushed to the market for tomatoes, and it never once

felt Hallmark-movie-esque. Maybe it was because it was missing the scene where I bump into a handsome stranger, causing the tomatoes to splatter into a hot, saucy mess on the floor, locking eyes and turning fifty shades of tomato-paste red. As a married woman, that's likely for the best. My point is that you are the main character of your own life, and it's time to start romanticizing your role. To do this, you need to slow down and engage all of your senses in every task.

Let's put this into practice. Take grocery shopping, for example. Sounds pretty basic AF. First, plan to shop when you won't be in a rush, so that you're not cramming it into the ten minutes between work and school pickup. Whenever there's an element of rushing involved, it's hard to stay present; you're focused only on finishing the task quickly in order to move on to the next. Rushing perpetuates future thinking. If you're constantly rushing to do things, you need to make more time to do them. Start by cutting out unnecessary tasks and scheduling the appropriate amount of time for important ones. Before listing all the reasons why you're busier than everyone else or why your circumstances are harder, remember that there are people with greater responsibilities who choose to slow down and live intentionally. Living in chaos is a choice, as is living in peace. By prioritizing time for grocery shopping, you create the perfect opportunity to practice being present and discover glimmers of joy along the way. Pause to appreciate these subtle wins and feel grateful for them. Engage all of your senses in the experience of grocery shopping—smell the fresh herbs, touch the fruits to feel their ripeness, observe the display of rainbow-coloured produce, listen to the background music, and taste any samples available. Grocery shop as if you're the one someone is watching in their favourite movie. You're the leading character in your life. Act like it!

Always look for glimmers of joy and engage as many senses as you can in every task. Make it a goal to infuse as much magic as possible into everyday moments. I never realized how magical mundane tasks could be until I learned that creating the magic was entirely up to me. Go ahead and try it. When doing laundry, feel the textures as you fold the clothes, smell the fresh detergent, appreciate how neat the folded pile looks, and listen to the subtle clinking of hangers as you hang your favourite pieces. You'll soon discover that even the most routine chores can become moments of unexpected pleasure.

One of my personal favourite mundane moments comes, unsurprisingly, from making a cup of coffee—French press, to be exact. It's not just a routine; it's a ritual steeped in anticipation and delight. This is an ode to my love affair with coffee...

There's something deeply spiritual about the manual process of making a French press coffee. It starts with the initial anticipation of indulging in the bold, steamy, soul-awakening beverage and continues with the delayed gratification of immersing oneself in the process. I hear the dull, subtle sound of the coffee beans rattling together as my hand scoops into the bag, firmly wrapping my fingers around an oversized handful of smooth, hard, silky shells.

Some beans slip through my fingers and back into the bag as I place them into my handheld grinder.

As I engage the lever, I can feel the grinder churning, creating tension between the blades and the beans as they surrender to the pressure and turn into coarse, earthy-looking particles. With each churn of the grinder, the vibration works its way up my wrist, reverberating through my arm and eventually throughout my entire body. I gently twist the glass jar off the bottom of the grinder, where the fresh grounds have gathered, and lift it to my nose, bracing myself for the best part—my favourite kind of aromatherapy. I take a slow, deep breath, inhaling the aroma of absolute perfection. It gives me goosebumps as the bold, rich scent fills my lungs and awakens my soul. Freshly ground coffee smells like pure energy.

I repeat the deep breath at least two to three times before relinquishing the grinds into my French press carafe and slowly begin to pour 195-degree water as I observe the grinds slowly blooming while they rise and bubble to the surface. Due to the long, sleek spout design of my kettle, it takes about 30 seconds for the hot water to fill the French press carafe. As it fills with steamy water, I take a moment to reflect on a few things I'm grateful for. On goes the top of the French press, and I set a four-minute timer on my phone, patiently waiting until I can press the fully saturated grinds to the bottom and finally experience "the pour." I grab my well-travelled coffee tumbler from the cupboard and set it aside.

Once my alarm goes off, I press the mesh plunger down. As the grinds are forced to the bottom, I take pleasure in the slight resistance on my palm as I steadily complete the full French press. I begin to pour the French-pressed coffee into my tumbler, and the rich fragrance infuses the air around me, wrapping me in a warm, invisible hug. Steam evaporates as the hot liquid fills my cup—both literally and figuratively. The sound of coffee pouring is like music to my ears, and the first sip is a symphony for my soul. As I wrap my hands around my favourite weathered tumbler and tilt it toward my lips, the steam gently kisses my face before vanishing into thin air, and it's love at first sip. The complex flavours invigorate my taste buds, sending a flash of hot liquid intensity surging through my entire body. Ahhhhhhh!

…And that's my daily French press coffee ritual.

"But what about the cream and sugar?" you ask…

To which I would reply, "Adulterated coffee? Absolutely not."

Black.

If you're reading this and wondering, I'm a Grande Pike Place, black (you know the place). See you soon!

You can see how by engaging all of your senses and immersing yourself completely in the full experience of any seemingly mundane task, it makes it impossible not to be present in the moment. By slowing down and savouring each passing moment as if it were the last, you open yourself up to a world of beauty and possibility. Every breath becomes a celebration, every action a form of gratitude.

Romanticizing the ordinary transforms everyday experiences into cherished rituals. It invites you to see the magic in the little things, from the warmth of your morning coffee to the gentle rustle of leaves in the breeze.

Life is a collection of moments—make each one count. Choose to live fully, intentionally, and passionately. What small, everyday moments will you transform into cherished rituals today?

Chapter Nine

SOCIAL MEDIA UNPLUGGED

I am of the generation who can actually (and very fondly) remember what life was like before social media—when phones weren't very smart at all but could simply make a call. These phones were attached to a wall via a cord that resembled the tail of a pig. It wasn't until I was about 14 years old that I got my very first Nokia cell phone, before upgrading a few years later to a pink Motorola Razr flip phone—a true status symbol of my teenage years. Back then, phones were primarily used to call people and maybe text if you had the patience to do so via a numbered keypad. There was no social media yet. Growing up without smartphones and social media was quite literally the best. I played outside, rode my bike everywhere, and my curfew was the illumination of the streetlights. I was able to create memories without a device distracting me and stealing my attention away from life's most precious moments. The best part is that there's no photographic evidence of all the dumb shit I did back then either—bonus! Unfortunately, kids today aren't going to remember much about their childhoods because they're not fully present or actively engaged in anything memorable; they're glued to their devices. This is the direction society hoped we'd head toward—a culture of device-addicted humans who cannot set appropriate boundaries with the virtual shopping channels in our pockets. A device from which we impulsively seek validation, gratification, and a false sense of confidence. It's pretty ironic that this little handheld device has gotten so out of hand.

I've fallen down the unconscious rabbit hole of social media a time or two (or three thousand) throughout my life. I've spent countless hours alternating between creating my own content and aimlessly scrolling, consuming everyone else's. I had subconsciously bought into the idea that social media was an essential part of living and thriving in the 21st century. I'd unknowingly absorbed the subliminal messaging these platforms fed into my mind, leaving me questioning, *What's the point of doing anything if it's not shared online for everyone else to see?* The absurdity of this question is painfully obvious when written in black and white, and yet it's something that the majority of society believes to be true these days. Is it a coincidence that people who partake in social media are called users—the same term coined for drug addicts? I don't think so.

It wasn't until I read a book called *Digital Minimalism* by Cal Newport that my perspective and relationship with social media completely changed. At first, when this book was recommended to me, I rejected it completely. Nothing about it sounded remotely interesting. I loved social media and definitely did not want to be convinced by some dude to minimize my use of it. Naturally, I knew the second that I rejected the idea, it meant that I needed to read it. I've learned over the years that when we have strong reactions to things that trigger emotional responses, it's usually an indicator of something we desperately need to embrace, work on, or unpack. I had tossed it on my bookshelf to marinate in dust for a few months while I stewed upon the idea that my own resistance to reading it meant that I should, in fact, read it. Eventually, once I felt bored enough to give it a try, I reluctantly brushed the dust off the top and cracked the spine to see what Mr. Newport had to tell me about my social media usage (insert eye roll here). My eyes went from rolling to scrolling, eagerly consuming the words, sentence by sentence. Part of me became prematurely annoyed at what I knew I needed to read, while the other part couldn't put it down. The concepts and explanations put everything into perspective in a way that I couldn't argue with or deny. To form well-rounded opinions, I often seek out opposing views and challenge all angles, which has sharpened my critical thinking skills over the years. However, when I tried to counter the points Mr. Newport made in his book, I couldn't find any opposing viewpoints despite my best efforts to defend my social media habits. Yet again, I found myself faced with new truths and concepts that I could not unlearn—another red pill vs. blue pill situation. After reading this book a couple of times, I soon realized that I would not be able to return to my previously compulsive social media habits because I now knew better.

Digital Minimalism is a book that I now recommend to everyone and continue to reread when I feel I need a reminder (or when my negative social media habits start creeping back in). This book helped me redefine my relationship with social media, set boundaries around it, and question whether the time versus value trade-off of using it is even worth it (spoiler: most of the time, it's not). Social media is a major time suck, and the author paints a compelling picture of how shallow and surface-level our social connections are on digital platforms compared to authentic, real-life, in-person ones. Social media gives us the illusion that we have lots of friends, when, in reality, we end up spending most of our time alone and isolated as we scroll—and there's nothing social about that.

The term social media is actually kind of an oxymoron when you think about it. A more appropriate name would be Isolation Media, but we all know that would never sell or attract users. It would definitely make more sense, though, considering social media prevents us from feeling the natural desire to actually go out and socialize by providing us with the false illusion that, by engaging in an online platform, we are socializing. Engaging in social media is not socializing. Socializing is interacting with the 3D world and physically engaging in social activities with other real-life humans. It involves face-to-face interactions and being fully present in the company of others.

Rest assured, I'm not going to tell you to kibosh your social media accounts altogether; however, if that feels right for you, I fully support it. I believe these platforms can be beneficial tools if used as such—tools. Not as replacements for living in the present moment, and most certainly not as substitutes for deep and meaningful friendships. There is nothing social about sitting at home alone in your underwear, interacting with a 2D world through a device with a screen. Contrary to the marketing propaganda that these platforms shove down our throats, they are not a replacement for real, in-person friendships. Don't let anyone convince you otherwise, or you'll be destined to live a very empty, unfulfilled life. To change our relationship with social media, we first have to peel back the misleading marketing claims and see it for exactly what it is. Social media is a form of cheap entertainment—the same quality we might find in the pages of a trashy gossip tabloid magazine.

In fact, it's essentially like having a television in our pockets, inundated with tacky infomercials, where we mindlessly tune into the reality shows of our so-called "followers" or "friends"—most of whom we've never met in real life—while they flaunt their "Sephora Hauls" or "Must Haves" from Costco. Unfortunately, many people don't realize that they could be much happier if they put their phones down and learned to romanticize life, enjoying the present moment instead of getting caught up in the endless cycle of likes, shares, and digital validation. It's impossible to be fully present while simultaneously documenting what you're doing; when you focus on capturing the moment, the act of documentation overshadows the experience itself.

Recognizing this challenge, I've found ways to incorporate social media into my life intentionally with the appropriate boundaries. If you follow me on social media, you'll notice that I occasionally document and share moments from my life. By setting proper boundaries, I've managed to do this without compromising life's most precious experiences. Below are seven tips on how I've integrated the best aspects of social media into my life without letting it distract me from being present and enjoying real-life experiences. Setting proper boundaries and significantly limiting distractions for extended periods has been essential for me;

without these measures, I wouldn't be able to write books or engage in deep, meaningful work. Here are my tips for incorporating social media into your life in a more balanced manner:

1. **Be Intentional with Your Moments:** You have to learn to be very intentional about what moments you choose to document and what moments you choose to fully enjoy and keep to yourself. Some moments are too precious to be interrupted by reaching for our phones, and let's be real, some meals are better enjoyed hot rather than lukewarm after being subjected to an obligatory photoshoot. Creating discipline with your content creation and learning to set healthy boundaries is the first step. Adjust the ratio of content creation vs. present moment enjoyment to reflect what's most meaningful and important to you. I hope that after reading this chapter, you find yourself prioritizing present moment enjoyment over a quick dopamine hit of superficial content creation. Remember, the memories we create in real life far outweigh any likes or shares, so strive to cultivate experiences that nourish your soul and foster genuine connections.

2. **Capture, Then Disconnect:** If you do decide to photograph or document a moment, I encourage you to capture the content and then put your phone away for the remainder of the time. Save the actual editing or posting of it for later when you have some downtime dedicated specifically to that. Don't waste more time at dinner with friends by editing,

posting, sharing, and engaging in comments for the rest of the night, otherwise you'll be completely checked out and not present the entire time. I understand the desire for documentation or a group selfie to capture the moment. However, I often see people glued to their phones for extended periods while out with friends, under-appreciating and devaluing the pure gift of each other's presence. When people make the effort to set time aside in their schedules to get together and connect in person, cherish it. Go ahead and take the photo, then put the phones away and share the gift of the present moment in the presence of people you care about. I promise that your followers won't notice or care that you didn't post in real-time.

3. **Plan for Content Creation:** I like to intentionally plan for content creation so that I don't feel obligated to capture every moment all the time. Plan for a specific date and time to create all of your content at once, and then, on the days in between, limit your phone and social media usage. Breaking the habit of constant creation will not only free up more time but it will also allow you to be more intentional in creating quality, well-thought-out content which generally performs better in the algorithms anyway. I'm intentional about when I create content and when I don't. For instance, I love to travel. On some trips, I dedicate myself almost entirely to content creation, photography, and videography. In contrast, other trips are all about prioritizing

family time and savouring the experiences for myself. If I know I'm heading to a spectacular location for content, I'll designate it as a "content creation trip," ensuring I pack all my gear, props, outfits, and equipment. On the other hand, there are places that I travel to where I choose to be primarily present (often places I've visited before, trips with friends, or landscapes I'm less interested in capturing).

4. **Customize Your Notifications:** Set up a custom do-not-disturb setting on your phone where you receive zero notifications except for the ones you choose while your phone is in this mode. I love this feature so much because I don't always feel like it's practical to turn off my phone entirely or to put it on the default do-not-disturb mode, where every single notification is turned off. Having my phone on and close by is just one of those things I've gotten accustomed to, and most of the time, shutting everything down creates anxiety rather than peace and quiet. Customize your own do-not-disturb mode to allow for calls or notifications from whoever you choose—your spouse or kids, for example. As I write this, my phone is in a mode I call "Writing Mode," which I turn on every time I sit down to write. Sometimes I even leave it on well after I finish writing for the day just to bask in the prolonged peace and quiet. In this mode, my phone only rings when my husband calls. I don't have kids, but if I did, I would probably include them for added peace of mind...but that's it. I don't get email noti-

fications, nor do I receive any social media dings, dongs, or buzzes. My phone doesn't ring if anyone other than my husband calls, and even he knows to only call when it's important while I'm focused on writing. Once I finish my work for the day and turn off Writing Mode, all of my notifications for the entire day appear at once. Occasionally, during a lunch or bathroom break, I will flick it off and on to check anything. You'll soon realize how unimportant and nonurgent most notifications actually are.

5. **Choose What to Engage and Disengage With:** Contrary to popular advice, I do not feel obligated to respond to all comments or DMs (or even emails, for that matter). The time vs. reward trade-off by doing this is not something I see value in personally. I only respond to things that I'm passionate about or genuinely interested in. So if I have forty emails proposing collaborations, podcast interviews, or business opportunities, I often will not respond to any unless I'm actually interested. I don't see much point in wasting time and energy replying just to say, "No thank you, I'm not interested," to forty different people. Though it might seem improper or impolite not to respond, choosing what to engage with prevents overwhelm and preserves my energy for more meaningful tasks. It also helps me to not feel pressured by any unanswered emails or DMs; they can build up all they want, and I don't feel constantly behind on replying to them because I know I won't be replying to all of them anyway. Plus, if

the people emailing or DMing really wanted me to be part of a project or collaboration, they should have made their pitch more exciting or convincing for me to want to participate in the first place. You may have heard the saying that if something doesn't evoke a definite "hell yeah," then it's an automatic "no." Well, that's how I feel when I read emails or DMs; I'm either really excited to respond with a hell yeah or I plead the fifth and allow my silence to speak on my behalf as a no. I'm not into being nice or polite at the expense of overwhelming myself, and you shouldn't be either. For the record, I do thoroughly enjoy engaging in authentic conversations from fellow readers so don't be a stranger. I'm sharing this because I know many of you can relate to feeling overwhelmed by the constant influx of requests. I just want you to know that if you don't feel compelled to respond, silence is an acceptable response, and it's not something to feel guilty or ashamed of.

6. **Protect Your Peace:** I ruthlessly mute or unfollow people that I am not excited to see pop up in my feed, and I block anyone who acts like a damn fool. My social media pages are mine, which means I get to decide who's invited to my proverbial platform party. If you think for one second that your ignorant troll ass is going to be gifted the "freedom of expression" on my posts, in my comments, or on my pages, then you are dead wrong. Get the hell outta here! I have no time to engage in hate or distorted opinions

on my pages, nor do I have time to hate on other people's pages. If you're disrespectful or distasteful, you're done. This doesn't mean that I don't welcome insightful, constructive conversations and healthy debates from people who have effective communication skills with positive intentions. However, just because I do, doesn't mean you have to. If engaging in debates or challenging conversations stresses you out, then block anyone who crosses that boundary for you. You get to set your own rules for your social media pages, and you should do so with your well-being as the top priority. If someone rubs you the wrong way or you don't feel like their intentions are genuine, just block them. Don't allow their negativity to continue driving you nuts every time you open the app. This is a rule every single person on social media should follow. You'd never invite someone into your home who disrespects you, annoys you, or makes you feel unworthy, so why would you tolerate that in your online space?

7. **Prioritize What Matters:** I prioritize my real-life friends, family, and things that are meaningful to me. I do not allow social media to distract me from the most important things in my life. It's easy to feel busy and overwhelmed with "too many things to do," leading you to avoid putting effort into the people and things that matter most. Let me show you where you can find all the "extra time" in the world that you feel you don't have. Go into the settings on your phone right now and pull up the "Screen Time"

setting. Here is where you'll see the exact amount of time you're trading daily, weekly, and monthly by engaging in superficial stimulation instead of prioritizing the people and things that matter most to you. This is a true reflection of where your priorities lie. Instead of saying that you don't have the time to do the things you wish you could, just admit that you're prioritizing wasting your life away on a digital screen with a bunch of weirdos on the internet who share videos of themselves going grocery shopping. It'll hit differently when you speak honestly to yourself, and I bet you'll start rearranging your priorities quickly when you begin telling yourself the truth. You can never use the excuse that you don't have time for something as long as your screen time displays *any* number.

Which of these seven tips will you start implementing today? Social media is not real life, and we need to stop over-glorifying it. I hope my above tips have helped to shift your perspective and that you've learned some tools that you can implement in your own life. Instead of using the number of followers, likes, shares, comments, or engagements as a measure of your value, consider this more accurate gauge: the amount of time you spend engaged in meaningful activities. Focus on the depth of your personal relationships and how fulfilled you feel with your life. The amount of followers you have speaks nothing to your character, nor is it a reflection of the value you provide to this world. If social media crashed and burned tomorrow, those numbers would prove to be as irrelevant and senseless as they truly are. I'd much rather live a life full of tangible moments in the presence of real people that I love and care about. Ultimately, true fulfillment comes from authentic connections and experiences that feed our souls, not from the empty pursuit of virtual validation. Less is most definitely more when it comes to social media engagement for me.

When discussing social media and creating boundaries around it in order to live a happier, more meaningful life, we can't ignore the addictive component that it has. It's important to know that it was created with the intent that we become addicted to it; thus, it's imperative that we don't engage with it carelessly. I've come across multiple articles referencing social media being compared to slot machines in how it manipulates the reward centres in our brains, making us addicted to the allure of its unpredictability. That urge you feel to compulsively check your phone to see whether or not you've got any new messages or notifications is the same impulse a gambler gets when they put their coins in the slot machine and pull the lever down. Every time you check your phone and there is a notification, you get a hit of dopamine the same way that a gambler does when they win something. It doesn't matter if you check your phone (or pull the slot machine lever) fifteen times with no notifications or winnings; just the possibility alone that on the sixteenth time you might receive something is enough incentive to neurotically keep checking your phone or pulling the lever.

When choosing to engage in heavily addictive activities, it's vital to set boundaries and limitations; otherwise, you run the risk of losing yourself in the addiction without even knowing it. Do yourself a favour and disconnect from as many apps as you don't need, and turn off any notifications that you can live without (which, let's be real, is most of them). Unsubscribe from useless emails. Unfriend and un-follow anyone who doesn't spark joy or add value to your life, and start to become more intentional and disciplined when it comes to checking your phone throughout the day. Practice leaving it in other rooms and not having it glued to your side. Sometimes I even plug my phone into a charger in another room and leave it there all day, pretending like it's an old-school phone with a cord from back in the day (bonus: by doing this, it actually encourages you to get up and move your body in order to answer phone calls). Set aside designated times to scroll and log in to social media with appropriate predetermined quantities of time, and hold yourself accountable to enforcing these measures. By implementing even a few of these new guidelines, it will help you to establish new habits and set better boundaries.

When it comes to social media, I can't help but pose the question of who is really benefiting from us using it? Is it us? Or is it the social media platforms, their CEOs, and the businesses who use it to market their products? If you guessed the latter, you'd be right. These platforms are designed to make money, and the more time that their users (AKA us) spend on these platforms, the more money they can charge companies for advertising to their users. In essence, they're exploiting you and me by free-labouring our time in exchange for cheap, low-grade entertainment and then making billions of dollars by doing it. The question we need to ask ourselves is why we're so willing to trade our most valuable asset—time—in exchange for something of such insignificant value. It's something to consider when deciding how much or how little to engage in social media. Sure, you might see a small return on your time investment if you run a business and use social media to convert customers, but have you ever stopped to consider how much time and energy it really takes to obtain that customer? You might be surprised to learn that if you do the math on that conversion rate, it might not be as good as you think. Having a business or brand presence on social media is definitely beneficial for most industries, but stop stressing yourself out over trying to keep up with the trends and recurring algorithm updates. The minimum that you have to do is maintain an aesthetically pleasing profile with a few posts throughout the week on a consistent basis. You don't need to be on every social media platform either. Just choose a couple that match the demographic of your target market and maintain those. A couple of well-maintained accounts are much better than a bunch of half-assed ones with no regularity. Focus your time and energy on creating and developing unique products and services rather than on an overproduction of useless content.

For example, with my previous cake business, I used social media to my advantage. It played a huge part in the growth and success of it, just not in the way you may think. Instead of spending tons of time and energy trying to figure out all the algorithms and wasting endless hours creating an overabundance of content, I focused my time and energy on the quality and creative design of my bakery products. By doing this, I was able to create extremely unique desserts that caught people's attention with only needing to post a simple photo or video of it because the dessert spoke for itself. All I had to do was post my creation, and it would naturally do well because people found it genuinely interesting. Thus, if you focus on making your business or brand more compelling, it will naturally stand out on its own and won't require too much extra time to be wasted on creating content. Standing out and making your business unique is the only real way to capture attention and convert followers into customers. So yes, social media can be a beneficial tool in growing your business if used intentionally, but it should still never be an excuse to use it in the absence of boundaries.

If you find yourself using social media solely for personal enjoyment rather than business, it's an even worse time vs. reward proposition. This underscores the need to establish stronger boundaries around its use. If this is the case and you're just using it as a means for cheap entertainment, then I encourage you to adopt a new hobby in lieu of at least *some* of the time you spend scrolling aimlessly. You don't have to give it up altogether, but do you remember that setting on your phone that tells you how much time you spend on your device that I was telling you about earlier? Start by dividing that time in half and use the other half of your newfound free time toward developing a brand new skill or hobby that you can fill your time with going forward. Your life will start to feel so much more meaningful just by simply replacing half of the time you waste on your device with a new hobby.

I have to share one of my recent and most profound smart-phone discoveries to date... Brace yourself for this discovery. Are you ready for it? Here it is… These devices actually have an off button! For real, for real. Did you know that? I was shocked when I found out that you can actually turn these little annoying Apple-Android fuckers off any time you want to. I couldn't believe it. Here I thought that I was a prisoner to this device and all its ding, dong, ring-a-ling glory this whole entire time. Do we own it, or does it own us? Seriously, it's silly to think that we allow these devices to hold so much power over our emotions and moods when we have the ability to silence them and give them a time-out in the junk drawer where they so often belong. I understand that it can feel uncomfortable to be disconnected and unavailable during rare emergencies when someone is trying to reach us, but taking short breaks of complete silence and disconnection can be incredibly refreshing. Social media has become so prevalent in our culture that we forget that we don't actually need it in order to survive. I remember the moment this hit me… It was one of those days when I tossed aside all my boundaries and was glued to my phone. I spiralled into frustration while wading through the ridiculous back-and-forth in the comment sections of one of my posts. You know the drill… getting caught up in arguments with people online whose opinions you'd never give a second thought to in real life. I remember thinking to myself, if I just turn my phone off, it would be so quiet and peaceful, and I could carry on enjoying my evening as per usual. So, I tried it, and… what a magical experience! The trolls disappeared into the Meta-verse (or interweb of oblivion—whatever you want to call it), and all was well. Consider this your reminder: your little smart-but-not-really-so-smart phone does, in fact, have an off button—so use it. We often forget this simple feature and underestimate the peace that comes from turning our phones off and enjoying moments of disconnected silence. The feeling of being constantly connected to the outside world 24/7 is just plain overwhelming. Unplug to recharge yourself for once.

The negative effects of constant scrolling are another detriment of chronic social media use to be aware of. If we haven't been diagnosed with an attention deficit disorder yet, we're about to inadvertently create one for ourselves. We are training our brains that it's not okay to sit in solitude without a device glued to our palm. We flinch at the slightest inkling of boredom, opting to prematurely alleviate it via access to our phones, whilst we aimlessly scroll. When we do this multiple times throughout our day, we end up getting to the point where we are unable to just sit with our boredom and be present in the moment. Though it might seem harmless to peruse your phone as you sit there, bored and waiting for your flight, what you're really doing is training your brain to bounce around from topic to topic as fast as your thumb can scroll. It inhibits your ability to focus properly in situations where you need to be able to focus later on. We're training the focus right out of our brains. It's why so many people find it nearly impossible to concentrate on one task for long enough to complete it. They end up frustrated and blaming themselves when it has more to do with their scrolling habits than it does with anything else. Learn to sit in boredom or at least use other means of entertainment that actually feeds your brain and assists in strengthening your focus, such as reading or listening to an audiobook.

In addition to the distractions of scrolling, it's equally important to recognize the impact of sharing content on social media. Before you hit that "Post" button, it's essential to recognize that you're opening yourself up to feedback, criticism, opinions, and perspectives from the public. It really doesn't matter what you're posting; there is always potential for someone to let you know how much they hate it. This can be a major wake-up (and smell the fucking coffee) moment when you were innocently just posting a cute video of your dog laying on your bed. How can this be triggering for some stranger on the internet? We will never know. It's not for us to figure out or understand. There are unhinged people out there. I think when people react so negatively to others, it's akin to having the human equivalent of rabies; their behaviour becomes a chaotic eruption of anger and hostility that feels utterly disconnected from our shared humanity. It's as if a dark cloud has descended over their souls, warping their perceptions and twisting their emotions into something toxic and irrational. In these moments, they unleash a torrent of bizarre and hurtful words, much like a rabid animal foaming at the mouth, spewing venomous remarks that not only shock but also sicken us. This irrational fury contradicts the very essence of what it means to be human—compassionate, understanding, and kind. It's a heartbreaking reminder of how far some can stray from the light of our shared humanity, turning into wild, unpredictable creatures driven by their own inner turmoil. They're unwell. Block them and be done with it. Trying to understand or analyze their bizarre behaviour is a waste of time and energy. The world is filled with what I like to call "characters of the world," and it is just something that we have to accept when choosing to participate in public platforms like social media. Most platforms these days have an option where you can turn off the comments section. Do it. Regain control back on your social media pages. I see a lot of celebrity accounts disabling comments and adjusting their privacy settings to suit whatever feels most comfortable for them, and I think it's awesome. Why the hell should we even care to hear other people's opinions flooding our comments sections anyway? Even if they're good? The good comments feed our egos, and the negative comments feed our insecurities. Neither helps us nor adds value to our lives in any way. You know why? Because these are strangers on the internet. It might seem harmless to indulge in all the glorious, ego-boosting comments; however, if you allow yourself to experience the emotional high of the positive ones, you'll also experience the emotional low of the negative ones when they occur (and they will). It's called duality. Until you can accept both compliments and criticism with minimal impact on your emotions, mood, and well-being, you will always experience the highs and lows that accompany such dualities. Learning to be stoic or unfazed by both the good and bad comments is where you want to be. It takes a lot of practice to get good at remaining neutral to both; however, by practicing it every chance you get (specifically with the good comments because they're a bit easier to neutralize than negative ones), you'll become less and less affected by anyone's opinion of you, one way or another. It's important to have grace with yourself as you practice this because there will be days when you're not in a great mood—maybe you're tired or sick—and if you're already in a lower state of mind, it will be much harder to prevent these comments from affecting you. When you're not in a great mood to begin with, it's best to stay off social media entirely. You're better off doing anything else—light chores around the house or enjoying some self-care. Social media is extremely rough on our mental well-being in general due to the plethora of content we expose ourselves to. Humans were never designed to handle the overwhelming volume, complexities, and sheer quantity of news and information that social media bombards us with daily. We lack the mental, emotional, and spiritual capacity to process everything that's going wrong in the world, and this affects us deeply, even if we believe we're tough enough to manage it. As human beings, our subconscious absorbs negativity at an alarming rate, and before we know it, this buildup manifests as anxiety, depression, and unhappiness. To counter this, we must disconnect from the chaos of social media to reconnect with ourselves. When you're not feeling your best, go make yourself a coffee, fold some laundry, listen to a podcast, or get outside in nature, and allow some unplugged time for yourself.

While social media can be a helpful business tool when used thoughtfully, it's essential to engage with it mindfully and with clear boundaries. I encourage you to take a step back and ask yourself a few very honest questions:

1. Why do you use social media?

2. What do you gain from using social media?

3. What are you missing out on because of the time you spend on social media?

4. What things do you wish you had more time to do
   in real life?

5. How much screen time does your phone say you
   use?

6. Is the time you're spending on your phone and social media getting you the tangible results you're
   looking for?

7. If you spent less time on social media, what else
   would you have time for?

I hope that by asking yourself these questions, you can
connect the dots to create a clear roadmap for where you
want to go from here and the type of boundaries you'll
need to set to get you there. While I have no intention of
ditching my phone or favourite platforms altogether, I've
completely redefined my relationship with them. I've set
new boundaries, and continue to be mindful of the value
versus time trade-off I get by engaging with my devices.
From reading *Deep Work*, I've learned that disconnecting
and immersing myself in meaningful, high-quality work
that serves others is far more fulfilling. Remember: the
journey to a life of purpose begins with the courage to
discern what truly matters, and it's anchored in the power
of choosing where you direct your attention.

Chapter Ten

LIVING AUTHENTICALLY IN AN INAUTHENTIC WORLD

Authenticity has always been inherently important to me for as long as I can remember. I'm not sure why, but I never had much of a desire to fit in, which is honestly kind of bizarre. Most people have a strong desire to fit in, or at least they can reflect on a period in their lives when they desperately tried. This is pretty common throughout elementary school and high school and, for many, lasts throughout their entire lives. As a kid, I remember trends coming and going, and I never felt any fear about not being "cool" enough. Sure, there were some trends that I gravitated towards because I genuinely loved them—Modrobe pants, Tamagotchi pets, and skin-tight Tommy Hilfiger overalls in Grade 8 (don't ask)—but most of the time, I was uninterested in liking things just because other people did. In fact, the more the general population liked something, the less interesting it became to me. I didn't understand why I would want what everyone else had. I enjoyed unique things. Sameness and plainness were boring to me. My mom always said that as a kid I'd never want to wear an outfit unless it had something on it. In other words, plain clothing without a character or embellishment on it was a no-go for me. When I look back at old photographs, I can't help but laugh at how little I cared about what anyone else thought. It's clear in photos of me wearing a Little Mermaid sweatshirt paired with Care Bear sweatpants. Not much has changed since then, except now I at least try to pair my more elaborate pieces with a solid item, so there's some level of cohesion happening. I vividly recall this one shirt I had to have when I was around 13. It was lime green with a dark green, 70s-style square pattern, a collar that folded down, and translucent yellow buttons going all the way down the front. I can picture it clearly, and I assure you that it was as hideous as it sounds. But my 13-year-old self loved it and proudly wore it to school with no regard for anyone else's opinion. I thought if someone didn't like it, they didn't have to wear it, but that wasn't going to stop me from embracing my eccentricity.

On another occasion, around the same age, I was strolling through the mall with my bestie (the thing to do in 2001) when we came across the most iconic shoes we'd ever seen. I'm talking 4" platform heels with strappy buckles, entirely coated in chunky, gritty silver glitter. Today, I'd refer to these as "stripper shoes," though my 13-year-old mind didn't get that reference. We tried them on, waddling around the store like we were auditioning for a freak show exhibit at the local carnival. "We'll take them," we told the sales lady (who I'm sure was fighting back laughter). The next day, we tucked the shoes into our backpacks and brought them to school, fully aware that neither of our parents would have allowed us to leave the house in such outrageous footwear. There we were, sitting in our grade 7 classroom at our modest Catholic elementary school, with glittery platform shoes strapped to our feet. No shame and not a care in the world. I thought those shoes were a work of art. I don't remember what outfit I paired them with, but I wouldn't be surprised if it was tear-away Adidas pants with the bottom two clasps undone for optimal visual shoe impact. If I recall, we lasted about half a day before we swapped them out for sneakers due to foot cramps. It's times like these when I think back and wish I'd cared a little more about what others thought.

My love for oddities wasn't limited to clothing—it spanned across all areas of my life. While my girlfriends gushed over Backstreet Boys posters, I was swooning over Weird Al Yankovic. I actually have a photo from my 12th birthday with an edible image of Weird Al on the cake. My pre-teen bedroom was plastered in tie-dye and retro sixties decor for no other reason other than—I simply liked it. Fast forward to today…I'm in my mid-thirties and still haven't developed a taste for fitting in. Don't get me wrong; I have a healthy desire for deep, meaningful social connections, but I would never sacrifice my own authenticity for anyone's approval. If you feel like you have to change who you are to fit in with certain people, they're not your people. Find new people who embrace your uniqueness and allow you to be your true, authentic self.

Confronting Bullying: The Authenticity Advantage

Embracing our most authentic selves becomes nearly impossible when we remain preoccupied with others' opinions. Judgmental people and bullies, often driven by their own fears and insecurities, create barriers that make it difficult for others to express their true identities. This dynamic fosters an environment where authenticity is suppressed, leading many to grapple with self-doubt and the desire for acceptance. At our core, we all share a deep desire to be true to ourselves and pursue what aligns with our innermost values. However, fear of judgment and the potential for ridicule often hold us back from fully expressing who we are. I have a very different opinion on overcoming bullies and judgments from others, and it has nothing to do with them and everything to do with us.

For all intents and purposes, I should've been an easy target for bullies. Thankfully (and somewhat surprisingly), I'd never been bullied. I mean, of course, I'd experienced isolated incidents of kids being mean here and there; no one is immune to that. But, I'd never been the victim of constant and relentless bullying, even though I had every reason to be. I was weird, strange, peculiar, awkward, and chubby. I embodied the characteristics of almost every kid in every movie that ever got bullied (minus the above-average nerdy, book-smart intelligence; that trait skipped over me). So how come I could be authentically weird as hell and get away with it in our modern, judgmental society? I wasn't entirely sure, but the more I pondered this question, the only reason I could conclude was that I simply didn't care what anyone else thought about my taste in clothing, music or really any other personal preferences. I didn't care if people didn't approve of the things that I enjoyed or whether they judged me for how I chose to dress or style my hair. Therefore, it seemed like no one found it fun or rewarding to bully someone who was unfazed by their judgments. Bullies tend to seek reactions, and their egos feed on the hurt feelings and emotional reactions of their victims. This got me thinking... What if we, as a society, have this whole anti-bullying campaign completely backwards? Instead of directing our efforts towards the bullies themselves in attempts to eradicate their behaviour, what if we directed our efforts away from the bullies and towards everyone else? We could aim to equip the general population with proper self-esteem, authenticity, strong communication skills, and an unwavering confidence to be who they want to be, irrespective of what anyone else thinks. While the campaign to end bullying sounds like a decent solution, attempting to target bullies in hopes to convince them to change their behaviour is pretty fruitless. After all, they tend to be completely oblivious to their de-structive behaviour patterns. Whereas the victims of bully-ing would be much more eager and responsive to adapting new strategies in the pursuit of ending bullying. I really want you to remember this quote of mine when it comes to bullies:

You can't bully a person who doesn't believe or value what the bully is saying.

Let that sink in for a moment. The only people who un-fortunately fall victim to bullies are the ones who believe or value what the bullies are saying. If they didn't believe it or value it, then it wouldn't hurt their feelings. They would just think that the bully is a negative or mean per-son, but it wouldn't have such a detrimental impact on their self-esteem or well-being, nor would it waver their self-confidence. Therefore, fully embracing authenticity and developing unwavering confidence to be oneself is the formula for repelling bullies. A bully bug spray, if you will.

No bully is going to continue bullying someone from whom they do not get a desired negative reaction.

I'm not talking about suppressing our feelings and pretending to be okay when our feelings get hurt. Instead, I believe that the more we learn about why people are mean in the first place—such as their own insecurities or unresolved traumas—the more genuine compassion and empathy we can have towards them. This understanding allows us to respond with kindness rather than defensiveness, thereby diminishing the negative impact of their behaviour on us. We must learn to let go of our innate desire to fit in or be liked, as doing so allows us to cultivate genuine relationships and a deeper sense of self-worth that isn't dependent on external validation.

Now, don't get me wrong; I agree that fewer bullies roaming the earth would be ideal, but let's face it, so long as there are hurt people with unresolved baggage in the world, bullies aren't going anywhere. They'll continue to show up on the playground, in workplaces, online, and in public. In case you haven't noticed, bullying doesn't just end in elementary school; it can show up in many places throughout life. So why not focus on the only thing that we can control—ourselves? The bullies don't give a shit about our anti-bullying campaigns; it's the people who have been affected by bullying who truly care about them.

Recognizing that bullies are unlikely to disappear, we must shift our focus to more effective strategies for dealing with them. I'm in favour of harsher punishments for bullying (especially online, in schools, and workplaces), considering that in the year 2024, there have been no significant consequences assigned to such behaviours. I also think bullying should be considered a mental illness of sorts in order for further resources to be allocated to appropriate therapies that can help resolve the insecurities and deep-rooted pain that's been embedded in these people with bullying tendencies. A mandate for face-to-face mediation, where proper communication is taught and fostered along with proper conflict and resolution skills, would be helpful. The more healed people in the world, the less bullying there would be. Also, educating the victims of bullying on the psychological and emotional baggage, pain, and immaturity that the bullies carry with them can help to curate a sense of empathy towards the bully while also learning not to take anything they say to heart.

Learning empathy is an underrated skill to develop. Being empathetic towards bullies does not mean that you approve of or agree with their behaviour; it means you can have compassion for the underlying issues contributing to their negative actions. I like to examine situations from different angles to come up with creative solutions, especially since the current anti-bullying campaigns aren't eliminating bullies anytime soon. Ultimately, when evaluating solutions to challenging situations, I always arrive at a place of personal responsibility rather than defaulting to a victim mentality. By cultivating empathy and embracing personal responsibility, we can foster a more compassionate environment that empowers everyone to take responsibility in breaking the cycle of bullying.

Additionally, the role of bystanders is crucial in addressing bullying behaviour. When bystanders choose to intervene or support the victim, they can significantly impact the situation and deter the bully. That said, I often see bystanders who have good intentions but resort to bullying the bully, which only perpetuates the issue of bullying. It's important to educate bystanders on how to respond effectively, whether it's by speaking up empathetically, reporting the behaviour, or simply offering support to the victim. Encouraging a culture of accountability among peers can foster a safer environment, making it clear that bullying is unacceptable and that everyone has a role in standing against it. By empowering bystanders, we can create a united front against bullying, leading to a more compassionate and supportive community.

Regardless of any techniques that we can develop to combat bullying, we must also recognize that how other people treat us often has little to do with us. Most of the time, how people treat us is a direct reflection of how good their day, week, or life is going. The nastier people are, the more shit they're dealing with. Once you know someone is negative, mean, or a bully, set strong personal boundaries around your interactions with them. Depending on your relationship with them, you could choose to cut them out of your life completely or, at the very least, significantly reduce your interactions with them. In such cases, if you can't remove yourself from their presence entirely (for example, a co-worker, family member you live with, classmate, etc.), then drastically limit all interactions with them. Do not initiate any conversations, and keep all communications short, factual, and direct.

Above all else, maintain your own level of authenticity and integrity at all times, and do your own internal work to be able to allow their negativity to roll right off you. In challenging external situations where I can't control how others treat me, I concentrate on what I can manage. I prioritize maintaining my inner peace and extending compassion and empathy to them, rather than futilely attempting to change their behaviour. This demands that I continually cultivate my emotional intelligence and consistently practice regulating my emotional reactions, particularly in situations that frustrate or hurt me. It's not always easy when faced with nasty people, but the more that we practice true self-confidence, develop emotional intelligence, and regulate our own emotions, the less upset we will be by other people's opinions and negative behaviours. Remember that self-care is also essential; taking time to recharge and reflect can help us stay grounded and resilient in the face of adversity. By nurturing our well-being, we can better navigate challenging interactions and emerge stronger.

We'll now shift our focus away from the complexities of bullying to the broader challenge of maintaining authenticity in an inauthentic world. The more that our world develops and evolves, the more difficult it becomes to maintain our personal sense of authenticity. It takes a lot of critical thinking and intentionality to stay true to our core values, which is not always easy to do when our attention is being pulled in a myriad of directions. It's not really the world itself that is inauthentic; the natural world itself is magical and beautiful. The inauthenticity stems from the intervention of humans who have developed our societies and shaped our cultures into what they are today. It's our human society that has created an inauthentic environment for us to live in, filled with hidden motives and impure intentions in attempts to control and direct our attention, energy, and money. Of course, human intervention isn't entirely a bad thing, because without it, we wouldn't have cities with grocery stores, homes with electricity, or vehicles (among many other things that most of our modern society values). You've probably noticed that it can be difficult to remain authentically true to who you are in our modern culture for so many reasons. I know that I have. All the advertisements tell us what we should need or want to become a "better version" of ourselves. On top of this external pressure, friends and family also impose their values and beliefs on us, acting as if they know better or that their way is the "right way." Additionally, our culture forces us into buying whatever they're selling, promising that it will make us "feel better, look better, and be better." How much of this resonates with you? Would you act the way you do, buy the things you buy, or believe the things you believe if you were alone on a secluded island without society to influence you? Reflect deeply on your answer to this question. Living authentically means that you are uninfluenced and, instead, very intentional about everything you do, say, believe, and buy.

<u>Drowning Under the Influence of Influence</u>

While we're on the topic of influence, let's talk about how we're living in a world where being an influencer is an actual job title these days. There's not much that's authentic about being an influencer or being influenced. Sorry, absolutely not sorry. I understand the appeal of being an influencer—the idea of receiving free PR products to promote on social media and getting paid to create content around specific items sounds like a dream job. I even dabbled in it myself before realizing how off-putting it truly was. Sometimes, you need to experience something firsthand to create enough contrast that helps you definitively recognize how unappealing it is.

Whenever there's a hidden motive lurking behind something, it reeks of inauthenticity, prompting us to question the true intentions of those involved. It's essential to always scrutinize the intent and engage our critical thinking skills before making any decisions based on recommendations from someone online or behind a camera. Influencing is one of the least authentic means of marketing because a lot of influencers pretend as if they're not getting paid or compensated for what they're promoting (even though most social media marketing policies state that they must be honest about it). As for the ones who are forthcoming about being paid, we still, as consumers, have to question if we want to trust someone who is accepting compensation for what they're promoting. Even if they genuinely like the product they're showcasing, their primary intent remains to sell it to you, rather than to help you make an unbiased, well-thought-out, and educated decision about whether the product is right for you. That would require discussing the negatives and non-selling features of said product, which nine times out of ten is conveniently left out of their sales pitch.

What's worse is when influencers are compensated to post an "honest" review. How honest do you think it's going to be when they're being compensated? Sure, review-style videos can be helpful in the decision-making process of purchasing products. However, unless both the pros and cons are being discussed, then I question the person's ability to formulate a legitimate opinion on whatever they're reviewing. When I watch review videos, I'm aware that compensation is often involved. I also make it a point to research and watch reviews from others who had negative experiences with the same product. Understanding these diverse perspectives allows me to see beyond the marketing hype and make a more informed choice. I don't allow the positive or negative reviews to sway my opinion one way or another, but instead, I gather the evidence from both perspectives and draw my own conclusion. It's called critical thinking. The more you develop this skill, the less you'll be influenced.

I think that influencer marketing is genius from a business perspective. It works exceptionally well when people on the internet (whom their followers feel like they know, like, and trust) show and tell their favourite products. It's an easy sell… but only because we're an easy target. We, as consumers, keep buying all the stuff that's cluttering up our closets, cabinets, and drawers and wonder why we're so broke and unhappy. Well, it's because more stuff just creates more clutter, not happiness.

This tendency to accumulate unnecessary items often stems from impulsive purchases, which are typically the least thought-out and most unintentional decisions we can make. Take a scroll through social media, and you'll see eager influencers enthusiastically showing you everything you never knew you didn't need and telling you why you "totally" need it. These purchases often arise from emotional triggers, such as wanting to fit in or feel a sense of belonging. A quick and effective hack to cut back on impulsive influencer purchases is to get offline. Sign out of social media, shut your phone off, and get outside. Spending less time online is always time better spent—so long as you're not swapping your social media addiction for another vice.

The bottom line is that you'll drive yourself (and your bank account) crazy if you give in to everything your favourite influencer says you "must have." Instead of blindly trusting everything you see, hear, and read online, put some deeper thought and intention into whether or not you need whatever it is that they're suggesting you can't live without. After all, you've lived without it for this long, haven't you?

As I touched on in the previous chapters, impulse purchases reflect a void we're trying to fill with short-term bursts of instant gratification and cheap hits of dopamine. This is not what we're striving for here. We're aiming for sustainable, long-term peace and happiness, aren't we? I sure as hell am, and I know you are too if you've made it this far in reading my book. At the very least, I hope that you begin to consider all the angles of what someone on social media is suggesting and learn to trust yourself to make your own decisions. Learning to trust yourself and your own abilities to figure things out is how confidence is created and maintained.

Just for the record, I don't think influencers are bad people with terrible intentions. I just think that influencer marketing has gone way overboard and is overly saturated in a culture that prioritizes consumerism over authenticity, leading to a cycle of impulsive purchases and empty promises. Most of these influencers just do it because it feels fun and pays well (if they have enough followers). Some of them probably genuinely love the products they're promoting. And I'm most certain none of them care about my personal opinion. They're just doing what society has ushered them towards because companies have figured out that influencer marketing is a more profitable marketing and sales strategy than most others these days, since the majority of consumers are wasting their lives away on social media.

Back when TV, radio, and newspaper commercials were the primary means of marketing, the ads were easier to dismiss and ignore because we didn't have the same connection to the companies trying to sell us products. In those days, ads felt more like interruptions. In contrast, today's online influencers build personal relationships with their followers. This connection creates a sense of trust and relatability, making their "helpful suggestions" feel more compelling, which can lead us to consider their recommendations more seriously. Influencers aren't going anywhere anytime soon and if we're going to be inundated with their product recommendations, it's important to be hyper-aware that their intention is to persuade us to purchase or endorse whatever they are promoting. My purpose of bringing this up is to remind you that we still have the power to choose how we engage with this content. We can decide to critically evaluate their recommendations rather than accepting them at face value, ensuring that our purchases align with our true needs and values.

As we navigate the emerging world of influencers, it's important to recognize that we all hold the power to influence those around us, often without realizing it. Each of us has the potential to influence our friends, family, and communities simply by the way we choose to live our lives. Every action we take, no matter how small, sends a message that can inspire others to reflect on their own choices and values. This innate human tendency to be influenced by one another is precisely why influencer marketing is so effective; it capitalizes on the trust and connection we naturally form with those we admire. I urge you to please use your influence with integrity and intention; strive to set a positive example rather than compromising your authenticity for monetary gain. Influence responsibly. The most effective way to inspire change is not through words, but through actions. When you live authentically and passionately, you naturally encourage those around you to do the same. Embrace your role as an influencer in your own right, and remember that your greatest impact comes from being the change you wish to see in others.

Evolving Authenticity: Embracing Change and New Beginnings

Developing our authenticity is one thing, but what happens to our sense of authenticity when we grow, evolve, and change? When it comes to maintaining our authenticity, we have to continue to reevaluate whether or not we are still in alignment with our values as we learn and grow throughout our lives. Nothing will lower our vibration, dampen our spirit, or dim our light faster than living our lives out of alignment with our most authentic selves. Though it might sound easy, I can assure you it requires a lot of regular reflection and mindfulness because, without being aware, losing your sense of authenticity can happen faster than your cognitive mind can keep up with.

That's what happened to me with my bakery business. I had slowly begun a journey toward health, wellness, and weight loss and was learning about all the negative effects of processed foods, refined sugar, artificial flavourings, and food dyes. As time went on, my passion for health and wellness grew while I tried to ignore the fact that I was running a million-dollar bakery business that was in complete opposition to this new lifestyle. Over time, I started feeling less and less passionate about my bakery business and even began to feel guilty about marketing and promoting my own products, knowing how harmful they were to the health and well-being of others. It took me far longer than I'd like to admit to realize that my waning passion was due to my newfound knowledge, which highlighted how my healthy lifestyle was completely misaligned with owning a bakery and selling cake. It felt deeply inauthentic—so much so that it started to feel painful. Authenticity has always been a core value of mine, and when I began to feel inauthentic, I knew that something had to give. I also knew that it wasn't going to be me abandoning my new healthy lifestyle.

This experience illustrates a larger truth about life: as we evolve, so too must our choices and values. Change is inevitable, and it often challenges us to reassess what truly matters. Self-development is a wonderful thing, and it's what allows us to become better versions of ourselves.

We just have to continue asking ourselves, as we grow, if what we are currently doing still matches our values or not. When our jobs, careers, relationships, or lifestyles start to shift and become a conflict of interest with our personal values, we must tune in and readjust by all means necessary. This requires a lot of self-awareness and courage, as it generally involves executing massive changes that may feel uncomfortable but are essential for reclaiming our authenticity and aligning our lives with what truly matters to us. Though I didn't really have much of a plan in terms of an exit strategy and had no idea what I'd do next, I felt that if I got rid of the cake business, realigned myself, and made room in my life for something new, then, in time, the Universe would present me with something bigger and better.

Spotting the Signs of Inauthenticity in Others

It's also important to identify inauthenticity in others, not so we can point fingers or call them out, but to foster healthier relationships and protect our own authenticity. The more authentic you become yourself, the easier it is to spot inauthenticity in others. Being authentic in friendships and relationships means that you can have different beliefs and opinions while still respecting others for having their own. I would much rather surround myself with truly authentic people than with those who pretend to be someone they're not for the sake of approval or acceptance. I don't need all my friends to believe the same things I do; I just need them to be genuine and true to themselves. As long as there is mutual respect to agree to disagree on certain things, I would much prefer someone to express differing opinions than to have someone who flip-flops their thoughts and beliefs for the approval of others. Authenticity and the ability to stay true to oneself are indicators of trustworthiness in people. For me, there's nothing worse than when someone tries to get close to you for some inauthentic reason, selfish objective, or hidden motive. I call these people "proximity parasites," where their only goal is to befriend someone based on superficial premises such as a large social media following, money, power, status, or to selfishly convert them into a sale within their business. These people will act like chameleons, blending their personalities to mimic yours by any means necessary in attempts to connect with you. They couldn't care less who you are, what you're into, or anything of genuine interest and will try to befriend you at all costs (including at the expense of their own authenticity). I can spot this happening from a mile away. Someone reaches out saying they'd love to get to know me and suggests grabbing coffee or lunch, only to pitch me or try selling me something mid-mouthful. It would be more authentic of them to just be honest and say that they'd love to discuss a business opportunity without slyly disguising it as befriending. There is a lot of confusion in the business world regarding how to effectively make connections and network. Many people attend networking events hoping to gain new clients or partnerships. However, instead of being clear and honest about their intentions, they may fake interest in personal topics, like your kid's soccer league, to capture your attention and build trust. Since authenticity has always been a strong value of mine, being in networking environments has always felt pretty cringey—from the superficial small talk all the way down to the fruit trays. I prefer to build genuine friendships and connections with people I truly enjoy being around first. If we later decide to do business or partner together, it will happen naturally rather than stemming from awkward, forced interactions over pineapple that's past its prime.

I crave honest, clear communication and loathe when people beat around the bush or engage in small talk while slyly sliding me their business card. Speaking of which, another thing to be aware of and honest about is your own motives. Always, always check your own intentions when trying to connect with people and ensure it's not for any externally selfish, hidden motive. I'll give you an example: Taylor Swift. She seems pretty interesting. Would you want to be friends with her? Most people would assume yes. But why? Is it because of what her status, social network, or net worth might be able to do for you? Or is it because you feel like you have a lot in common and would actually be lovely friends? What if you soon realized that after meeting her, you had nothing in common and she wasn't at all who you thought she was? Would you stop being friends with her? Or would you continue just because of who she is and what she has? If you did end up being genuine friends for the right reasons, you'd never imply or request access to her status, social network, or money anyway, because that's not what real authentic friends do. This is why people of status and celebrities have a challenging time cultivating genuine connections: because people want to be close to successful people for all the wrong reasons. It's also why they generally befriend others of similar social status, as there's less of a gap in perceived equity. Befriending Taylor might sound like a grandiose example; however, this happens all the time on smaller scales. Beware of people who don't come across as authentic or who do not contribute equal or greater value to your personal, business, or romantic relationships.

By the way, there's nothing fundamentally wrong with business deals or partnerships. They can be wonderful. However, they should be done in a very open, honest, and authentic manner where everyone is on the same page at all times. A little word of advice when attempting to partner, collaborate, or work with another human being—the best deals are when both people feel that they're getting the best deal. Most people think deals should feel 50/50, but really, I think they should feel like 100/100. Never accept a deal that doesn't feel like the other person has your best interest in mind, and never offer a deal where you aren't over-delivering value to the person you're hoping to work with. Only people who suffer from scarcity mindsets will offer you a deal that is better for them than it is for you (and still try to spin it in a way that makes it look like it's better for you). You'll want to stay far, far away from those people. Abundant people are extremely generous with their time, resources, and offerings. In the ten-plus years of running my bakery business, I've encountered many situations where people wanted to befriend me for inauthentic reasons and tried to rope me into deals that were glaringly more beneficial for them than for me. It taught me a lot about human behaviour and what to watch out for. It also taught me a lot personally about how I never want to come across like that to others. It helped me to solidify my own authenticity and boundaries while being able to respectfully reject ignorance disguised as opportunity.

I can't tell you how important it is to honour your own authenticity. It's the key to attracting everything you've ever wanted in life. Without embracing your own authenticity, you cannot attract the right friends, partner, career, or anything else that your heart knows you want but aren't brave enough to admit. One of the walls in my art studio at my house has giant wooden letters that I glued onto it that read: "The world needs who you were made to be." This quote serves as a daily reminder that we are all unique and that by unleashing our authenticity into the world, it is not only beneficial in attracting things that align with us, but it also serves others in a way that only we can do. The world needs it. The world needs you. The best part is that the more authentic you show up, the more other people feel comfortable showing up as their most authentic selves too.

The ripple effect of authenticity is infinite.

Brené Brown summed up authenticity in a beautiful quote that I'll end this chapter with in hopes that you embrace and implement it starting today: "Authenticity is the daily practice of letting go of who we think we're supposed to be and embracing who we are."

Chapter Eleven

WAKE UP AND SMELL THE COFFEE

Are you awake yet? Please tell me you can at least smell the coffee? And definitely don't tell me, after all this time, that you're one of those (insert eye roll) tea drinkers. I'm just kidding. I like tea too, but somehow I don't think "Wake Up and Smell the Tea" had the same bold ring to it. It sounds a little watered down, if you know what I mean…

I'm so grateful that you chose to take the time to read my book. You've learned about the most important lessons and strategies that have shifted, impacted, and realigned my life to feel more authentic. Everything that I've written about in this book has substantially influenced the way that I show up in my own life, and it woke me up in a way that I'll be eternally grateful for. I hope that it's done the same for you. I'm sure there were parts of this book that you read that you can't wait to start implementing, and other parts that seem a bit overwhelming for where you're at right now. Don't overwhelm yourself, but also, don't do nothing. I didn't learn all of these incredible lessons overnight. Some of them have taken me years to fully grasp their concepts prior to their implementation. Be gentle with yourself, because many of these lessons can take a few attempts and failures before they stick. Quitting wine, cutting out sugar, limiting my shopping, and learning detachment were among four of the most challenging ones for me.

Whatever you choose to change, whether big or small, I'm so proud of you! Change takes great courage. It's so much easier to keep doing what you've always done, especially when the entire world glorifies and reinforces mediocrity. Whenever you feel conflicted, unaligned, inauthentic, or like you just need the comfort of reading words from someone who understands what it's like to feel all of those things, I hope you'll reach for this book again or send a message to connect with me.

Writing this book has made me realize just how far I've come, and I don't know what the point of learning all these profound insights would have been if it weren't to share them here with you. I believe that you picked up this book for a reason (or maybe it was gifted to you by a friend). Either way, the Universe brought it into your life, and you had the courage to open it. Don't let the final page close without making a promise to yourself to reevaluate your own life and commit to realigning yourself with your inner purpose. It's a blessing to outgrow things and a sign that our lives are moving in the right direction—onward and upward!

When I made the decision to close down my million-dollar bakery business that I'd worked so hard to build over the last decade, I knew people would have opinions. They'd be upset, judge me, unfollow me, and probably think that I was nuts. I could've let the fear of their opinions keep me from closing, but their judgments were a reflection of their own limitations and stunted growth, not mine. I had to tune out all the noise and tune into what I knew in my heart was right for me. I'm convinced that if I hadn't outgrown my bakery business, I wouldn't have learned half of the lessons I've shared with you in this book, and truthfully, I can't envision living my life without them now.

The reality is that everything in our lives will come to an end at some point, including our own existence. So why not deliberately cut ties with careers, people, places, and things that we've outgrown? By doing so, we can realign ourselves and welcome more fulfilling opportunities. This way, we can make the most of whatever time we have left on this earth. I can't imagine wasting one more minute of my life begrudgingly saying yes to things I know I'll dread, putting effort into relationships that aren't reciprocated, doing work that's uninspiring, or being persuaded to conform to societal norms that breed unhealthy and unhappy people. Our hourglasses are steadily draining, each grain of sand a reminder that our time on this earth is finite and irrevocable. Once they've run out, we don't have the opportunity to flip them back over and begin again.

What are the things that you're going to stop wasting one more minute of your life doing?

In my previous book, *The Million Dollar Bakery*, I ended it with a chapter dedicated to creating the life of your dreams. I love this concept so much, but one thing that I've learned since then is that our dreams should continue to grow and change as we do. We have to embrace Wu Wei and go with the flow as we evolve, and we must allow our dreams to do the same. Creating the life of our dreams is not just something that we do once and then we're done. Creating is a verb. It's an action word, meaning that by creating the life of our dreams, we are constantly in motion as we continue to create, readjust, and recreate. It is a never-ending process. If you no longer love the life you've been creating up until this point, guess what? You get to create something new! Every day is a new opportunity to change directions if you want to. Embracing your own authenticity will lead you to the life of your dreams much quicker and more efficiently than in any other way. All opportunities that are meant for you can only find you if you're actively living your most authentic life. Without embracing your own authenticity, you will continue to attract unaligned opportunities that will keep teaching you lessons in attempts to wake you up to smell the coffee. I hope that by reading this book, I've helped you begin your awakening process.

As this book concludes, I'd like to remind you of your own ability to create a life that feels good to you without feeling obligated to blend in and enmesh yourself with an unconscious society. If you've made it all the way to the end of this book, I know that you have what it takes to step into your individuality and relinquish any previous fears of being too much, too loud, too weird, or too bold. Be all that you are. If people can't accept you for being everything that you are, allow them to go and find less somewhere else.

The thing about making changes in our lives is that it creates this forward motion of energy that's impossible to contain, and it ends up overflowing into other areas of our lives too. This momentum can spark creativity, deepen relationships, and open doors to opportunities you never imagined. All it takes is our commitment to take the first step in the right direction. Once you experience the benefits of creating healthy habits and living an intentionally crafted life that's authentic to you, there's no going back. You can't unlearn it, and you sure as hell won't want to once you experience how alive you'll feel. Embrace the journey of transformation; each small step compounds over time, leading to profound shifts in your overall well-being and fulfilment.

Currently, as I write this, I'm about ten months into my new bakery-free life, and there hasn't been a single moment of regret. I'm back to being fully aligned, continuing my health journey, and pursuing writing, photography, travel, art, and living authentically. I have loved slowing down this year and savouring the present moment. It has been a blessing to create my own routines and schedules, free from the chaos and disruption of the responsibilities that accompany running a million-dollar business. I won't miss the frantic phone calls from staff saying that they've run out of butter. Nor will I pine to answer another call from a customer complaining that their cake was missing one star-shaped sprinkle on the bottom left-hand corner. I've attracted so many aligned opportunities this year and have been able to practice turning down everything else. This summer marked the first time in over ten years that I could truly enjoy being present with my husband, friends, and family, free from the stress of fulfilling a huge volume of wedding cake orders every weekend. My husband and I took up a new summer hobby together: paddleboarding. I can't tell you how invigorating it has been to spend the weekends offline with our feet submerged in the cool Canadian lakes while soaking in the hot summer rays. I love sitting in peace and silence with all my senses engulfed in nature without the feeling of being needed by anyone. I often have moments where I forget that I no longer have to worry about all the business responsibilities, and it overwhelms me with gratitude.

The biggest lesson that I've learned this year is to slow down and enjoy the journey of any pursuit, especially the journey of life itself. Writing this book has taught me how to do just that. My writing process this time around has been the most enjoyable for me because instead of putting pressure on myself to publish this book as quickly as possible, I've allowed myself to enjoy and prioritize so many precious moments in between. From date nights, paddleboarding adventures, home exchanges, travelling, exploring, BBQs with friends, weekend getaways, to much-needed introverted solitude time by myself. In other words, I learned to fit my days of writing and editing into my life, and not the other way around. In the past, I'd always hustled and rushed toward the end goal of anything that I would set out to achieve, as if it was going to provide me with some spectacular feelings of worthiness or accomplishment. I'd tell myself that once I'd achieved whatever goal I had in mind, *then* I'd be happy, *then* I'd consider myself successful, *then* I'd be fulfilled. The "if this, then" mindset is one of the greatest illusions to plague our existence. Our ability to feel happy, successful, and fulfilled has to come from feeling these things in the present moment, wherever we're currently at, and not from an externally met goal or achievement. If you pay attention to the achievements in your own life, you'll notice that you never truly feel happy, successful, or fulfilled forever as a result of any one accomplishment.

One of the biggest takeaways that I hope you've gained from this book is the ability to apply critical thinking skills to your own life and question if the habits and behaviours you're currently exhibiting are contributing to a life that feels fulfilling to you. Not to your spouse, kids, boss, best friend, mom, sister, brother, dad, or mother-in-law, but to *you*. For most of my life thus far, I hadn't given much thought to societal conditioning until I started to broaden my perspectives and see just how normalized it was to be living an overindulgent, unhealthy, mediocre, mundane, miserable life. I began asking myself why I'd want to actively participate and engage in behaviours that lead to such negative consequences. The more I tried to make sense of it all, the less sense it actually made, thus leading me to pause one morning, and in lieu of sipping my coffee, I decided to wake up and smell it.

This awakening brought me to a profound realization—authenticity is a ripple effect of the highest magnitude of beauty. We have the power to create the initial ripple by expressing our own authenticity. Like a single droplet falling onto a still pond, the ripple begins small and barely noticeable. Yet as it travels outward, it grows in size and strength, reaching further and further until it touches every corner of the water's surface. This gentle expansion illustrates how our authentic expressions can inspire others, creating a chain reaction that amplifies our impact and fosters a wider community of genuine connection.

Have you ever felt an unshakable urge to change the world, only to be struck by the daunting thought that such a colossal goal might be forever out of reach?

Authenticity is how you can do your part in changing the world.

When we dare to be our true selves, we inspire others to rise into their own authenticity. One of the most profoundly rewarding experiences for me is witnessing others feeling truly comfortable being their authentic selves in my presence. Together, we can create a powerful community of support and inspiration, where authenticity thrives and everyone is empowered to shine. This connection fosters an environment where vulnerability is celebrated, encouraging us all to step out of our comfort zones and embrace the beauty of our individuality. Let us commit to showing up authentically, sharing our stories, and creating spaces where everyone feels valued.

It starts with us.

We must take the initiative to make the first move, creating a safe haven for others to follow. By cultivating this space, we transform our own lives and ignite a movement that challenges societal norms, inviting others to join us on a journey of self-discovery and acceptance. As we embrace our true selves, we not only undergo personal transformation but also help create a world that celebrates diversity and embraces our differences. There's nothing I love more than being around people who are confident in themselves and who can appreciate me for being myself, too. In this shared space of genuine connection, we unlock the deepest forms of love and belonging, creating a powerful force for change in the world.

Authenticity isn't just about allowing people to be themselves; it's about embracing their right to express themselves, even when our views differ. It means holding space for diverse opinions and recognizing that these differences can enrich our lives and perspectives. To love someone authentically, we must approach conversations with an open heart and mind, actively listening without judgment to understand the experiences that shape their viewpoints. Empathy is crucial for understanding those whose views may be dark or harmful, as these perspectives stem from deep pain, trauma, or ignorance. Recognizing the experiences that have skewed their understanding of the world allows us to foster compassion instead of judgement. By seeking common ground in shared values, we can use empathy to bridge the gaps between us. In order to create a space where people can be authentic and express their views—no matter how different their views may be—we must prioritize love, empathy and compassion. While it's important to respect everyone's right to share their opinions, we also have a responsibility to challenge harmful beliefs constructively. This involves engaging in open and honest conversations where we listen actively and seek to understand the underlying pain that influences their perspectives. By responding with empathy rather than anger, we can help them reflect on the impact of their words and beliefs. Establishing clear boundaries against hate and violence is crucial, but it's equally important to highlight that love and compassion can serve as powerful antidotes to darkness. Disagreement is natural. We can still respect each other while holding different beliefs. Fostering an environment of empathy and kindness creates a space where dialogue thrives and connections deepen, reminding us that our ability to love transcends our differences. Ultimately, authenticity invites us to celebrate the unique tapestry of humanity, recognizing that it's in our diversity that we find strength and understanding. In doing so, we contribute to a more compassionate world where healing and growth become possible for everyone.

We cannot afford to wait to start making a difference; life is fleeting, and every moment counts. Each day presents us with a new opportunity to embrace change and make an impact. Life is not permanent, and we have to stop living as though it is. The longer we linger somewhere that we've outgrown, the more resistance we'll face until we redirect ourselves. Resistance is that nagging feeling that tells us we're no longer aligned with our true selves; it's the discomfort that arises when our current circumstances no longer fit who we are. I want you to pay attention to when resistance shows up in your life and view it as a gift because when we're being too narrow-minded or complacent, it shows up to help us realign and change directions. It's a powerful signal from our inner selves, urging us to reflect and reconsider our paths. Resistance pushes us to confront our fears, question our choices, and ultimately break free from the confines of the familiar. Rather than fearing it, embrace it as an essential part of your growth journey. Every moment of resistance is an opportunity for transformation, inviting us to explore new avenues and awaken our soul's purpose.

Society as we know it, is a man-made construct that forcefully yanks us from our natural ways of being, tearing us away from our fundamental human nature. This leads to a lifeless existence, marked by monotony and disconnection, where days blend into one another without meaning or passion. It feels like slogging through fog, each moment heavy and uninspired, devoid of joy or excitement. Dreams and desires lie buried beneath layers of routine, stifled by fear and conformity. Emotions are muted, like colours washed out from the sun. In this existence, interactions are shallow, and the spark of genuine connection is absent, creating an echoing silence that amplifies a sense of isolation. It's a life that exists but lacks true vitality, yearning for purpose and vibrancy while remaining trapped in the shadows of unfulfilled potential. The rigid structures and expectations imposed by society overshadow our innate desires for connection, authenticity, and harmony. To find true peace on Earth, we must seek a better balance between the demands of modern life and the fundamental essence of what it means to be human. This journey calls for us to reconnect with our instincts, nurture our relationships, and cultivate a deeper understanding of ourselves and others. By doing so, we can embrace our shared humanity and foster a sense of belonging that surpasses societal boundaries. I believe we are meant to fulfill a greater calling during our time on this earth, and getting trapped in this work-hard, buy-shiny-things, retire-and-die societal shitshow will most definitely prevent us from achieving it. Let's rise above societal limitations and unleash our true potential, because the journey toward authenticity and connection isn't just a road we travel—it's a legacy we establish for ourselves and future generations.

From Vision to Reality: Building Your Authentic Life

Now it's time for you to put everything you've learned throughout this book into action. Take a moment to reflect deeply so you can create a blueprint and develop an action plan to help you on your way to creating the life of your dreams. Go ahead and envision the most authentic, intentional, and highest version of yourself right now. Do not allow any limiting beliefs, societal preconditioning, or imposed cultural views to slip in. I only want you to think about the ideal, best version of what you want your life to look like. Here are a few questions to get you started:

- What are you doing for work?

- How are you living?

- How are you spending your free time?

- What kinds of people are you attracting into your life?

- What is your romantic partner like?

- What habits do you have?

- How does your life feel?

- What are you choosing to spend your time, money, and energy on?

Now, take a moment to reflect on your life as it is today and ask yourself this crucial question:

Would you trade the life you're living right now for the one you just envisioned?

I hope it's a definitive yes. If it's not, it may be time to confront the reality that you didn't dream big enough and instead you allowed your current circumstances to overshadow your vision. Remember the powerful quote from Brianna Wiest I mentioned earlier in this book: "Your new life will cost you your old one." Embrace that truth—it won't come without sacrifice, but the reward will be immeasurable if you're brave enough to take the leap. You have the power to break free from limitations and step into a life that resonates with your deepest desires. This is your moment to choose courage over comfort and pave the way for a future filled with authenticity and fulfilment.

In order to become something greater, we must start living as if we are already that person right now, even though we aren't yet. This means adopting the mindset, behaviours, and routines of the individual that we aspire to be. For instance, if we dream of being more confident, we need to take bold steps today, such as speaking up in meetings, initiating conversations with strangers, or practicing public speaking in front of friends. If we envision a healthier version of ourselves, we should prioritize healthy eating, incorporating more wholefoods into our diets, and commit to regular exercise. If we aspire to be more organized and productive, we can start by setting daily goals, decluttering our living space, or using tools like planners and to-do lists to structure our time effectively.

By embodying these traits and habits today, we signal to ourselves and to the Universe that we are ready for growth. Though the change will not be immediate, each deliberate action aligns us more closely with our desired self, gradually shaping our reality. Over time, these consistent efforts will lead to the transformation we seek, allowing us to step fully into the person we aspire to become. It's impossible to get to our desired outcome without changing our daily routines to reflect the person that we want to become. I can't wake up one day and just decide that I'm going to be a bestselling author without engaging in daily writing practices. Athletes can't wake up one day and just decide that they're going to go to the Olympics without engaging in daily health and fitness practices. You can't become something without embodying it and being it now; transformation demands action today, not just dreams for tomorrow.

What daily habits will you start incorporating today to help get you closer to the person you want to become? Take some time to write out a daily routine that provides a clear plan for you to follow. I personally use the notepad on my phone to create a list with checkboxes, allowing me to mark off tasks as I complete them throughout the day.

As you prepare to embark on your journey of implementing these concepts, there are a few important steps I need you to take:

1. **Action:** I need you to take action the moment you

close this last chapter and start making clear-cut changes in your life. There are always those people who read books just for the sake of reading them. That's not what self-development books are for. They are to be used as a tool to help you progress further along your journey. Don't be that person and don't waste this opportunity to change your life. Remember, transformation begins with the first step. Whether it's setting a daily goal, establishing a new routine, or simply shifting your mindset, every action counts. Embrace this moment as the catalyst for your growth. The time for change is now—commit to it, and watch how your life begins to unfold in ways you never imagined.

2. **Grace:** Changing habits that have been ingrained in us for long periods of time is not easy to override with new, healthier habits. Expect to be challenged, but for the love of God, do not quit. Make mistakes and fail, but don't let quitting be an option. Have grace with yourself as you stumble, and do not strive for perfection. Remember that growth is a journey, not a destination. Each misstep is a learning opportunity that brings you one step closer to your goals. Just keep getting back up to try again. Everything that starts out hard gets easier over time, and the only way you'll be able to fail completely is if you stop trying altogether. Celebrate your progress, no matter how small, and remind yourself that resilience is built through perseverance. Embrace the imperfections, and trust that

every effort you make is a step toward the person you are destined to become.

3. **Share:** As an author who pours her heart and soul into her writing in hopes of helping to improve the lives of others, I would be incredibly grateful if you could share this book with your circle of friends and family. Your support not only helps me spread my message about living an intentional and authentic life, but also has the potential to inspire positive changes in the lives of those you care about. Change is often sparked by conversation, and by sharing this book, you could be the catalyst for someone else's journey toward growth. I genuinely want to hear your thoughts—what takeaways resonated with you the most, and how do you plan to implement these concepts in your life? Your insights mean the world to me, and connecting with my readers is the type of social media engagement I actually enjoy partaking in. You can connect with me on Instagram: @rebecca.hamilton.co or via e-mail: rebeccahamiltonco@gmail.com. Together, let's create a community that supports and uplifts one another on our paths to authenticity and fulfilment.

Finally, this is your reminder that you're never too old or too young, and it's never too soon or too late to change your life. You're exactly where you're meant to be, and it's not a coincidence that this book came into your life when it did. Do not revert back to living your life on autopilot, or you'll be flooded with regret at the end of it. I hope this book has ignited a fire within your soul to take an inventory of your life and commit to a path of rediscovering who you were meant to be.

I called this book *Wake Up and Smell the Coffee* because I want it to serve as your wake-up call to life. I want you to stop following the crowds and start following your heart.

Take this book as a metaphorical alarm clock blaring and penetrating deep into your soul, shaking you from the suffocating grip of the monotonous slumber you've been coerced into. Let its message reverberate through your very being, stirring every dormant dream and every flicker of passion you thought was dead. This isn't just a gentle nudge; it's a wake-up call to your true potential—a loud declaration that you deserve more than a life spent in the shadows of a sick, overworked, miserable society that glorifies complacency.

It's time to embrace the rich aroma of possibility, the invigorating scent of your dreams simmering just beneath the surface. The world is waiting for you to rise, to ignite that spark within, and to live fiercely, unapologetically, and authentically.

This is *your* moment to wake up and smell the coffee!

About the Author

Rebecca Hamilton is an award-winning entrepreneur and trailblazer in personal growth and wellness, inspiring others to reclaim their lives and reach their fullest potential. After closing her million-dollar bakery business, recognizing it no longer supported her new-found commitment to a health and wellness-focused lifestyle, she embarked on a profound weight loss journey, redefining her path with unwavering integrity, authenticity, and kindness. As the host of the transformative podcast Scrap the Sweet Talk, Rebecca engages her audience on powerful topics of self-discovery and empowerment. A passionate writer, she uses her work to connect deeply with others on their journeys. Outside of her mission-driven work, Rebecca enjoys hiking, photography, travelling, and immersing herself in the arts. She also loves spending time with her husband and their two dogs and finds joy in connecting with people from all walks of life.

Recommended Reading: My Favorite Books

Personal Growth and Transformation

- *Girl, Wash Your Face* by Rachel Hollis Encourages readers to let go of excuses and pursue their dreams unapologetically.

- *Girl, Stop Apologizing* by Rachel Hollis A practical guide for building confidence and breaking through limitations.

- *Build the Life You Want: The Art and Science of Getting Happier* by Oprah Winfrey and Arthur C. Brooks Insights into cultivating happiness and fulfilment through personal and scientific perspectives.

- *The Light We Carry* by Michelle Obama A motivational look at resilience, courage, and personal growth.

- *The Gifts of Imperfection* by Brené Brown Encourages embracing vulnerability as a pathway to wholehearted living.

- *You Are a Badass* by Jen Sincero A motivational guide for building confidence and embracing life with purpose.

- *From Strength to Strength* by Arthur C. Brooks Insights on embracing the transitions of later life and finding fulfilment in aging.

Mindfulness and Spirituality

- *The Power of Now: A Guide to Spiritual Enlightenment* by Eckhart Tolle

- *A New Earth: Awakening to Your Life's Purpose* by Eckhart Tolle Foundational texts on living in the present and cultivating deeper self-awareness.

- *The Universe Has Your Back* by Gabrielle Bernstein A guide on finding strength through spiritual guidance and trust.

- *Think Like a Monk* by Jay Shetty Offers principles on cultivating mindfulness and self-mastery inspired by monk philosophy.

Minimalism and Intentional Living

- *Love People, Use Things* by Joshua Fields Millburn and Ryan Nicodemus A thoughtful exploration of minimalism and changing our relationship with possessions.

- *Digital Minimalism: Choosing a Focused Life in a Noisy World* by Cal Newport Insights on managing digital distractions and living a more intentional life.

- *Deep Work: Rules for Focused Success in a Distracted World* by Cal Newport A guide to cultivating deep, focused work and improving productivity in a distracted world.

Health and Wellness

- *The Blue Zones: Lessons for Living Longer from the People Who've Lived the Longest* by Dan Buettner A research-based look at the world's healthiest communities and their longevity secrets.

- *The Easy Way Series* by Allen Carr

  - *The Easy Way to Stop Smoking*

  - *The Easy Way to Quit Emotional Eating*

  - *The Easy Way to Control Alcohol*

  - *Lose Weight Now* Practical approaches to overcoming habits and fostering healthier choices.

- *Good Energy* by Casey Means and Calley Means Insights on how to harness energy and optimize health.

- *Women, Food, and Hormones* by Sara Gottfried A comprehensive guide to understanding women's health through the lens of hormones and nutrition.

- *Heal Your Body* by Louise Hay A classic guide on the connection between mind and body for holistic healing.

- *The Emotion Code* by Dr. Bradley Nelson A guide to identifying and releasing trapped emotions for physical and emotional well-being.

Coping with Loss and Grief

- *The Grief Recovery Handbook: The Action Program for Moving Beyond Death, Divorce, and Other Losses* by John W. James and Russell Friedman

- *The Grief Recovery Handbook for Pet Loss* by John W. James and Russell Friedman Compassionate guides for processing grief and finding healing after significant loss.

Business and Entrepreneurial Journey

- *The Million Dollar Bakery* by Rebecca Hamilton The author's inspirational journey of building a bakery business from the ground up and how to turn your hobby into a million dollar business.

- *The Artist's Way* by Julia Cameron A creative journey to help unlock artistic potential and self-expression.

- *The War of Art* by Steven Pressfield Insights on overcoming creative blocks and achieving one's purpose.

- *Big Magic* by Elizabeth Gilbert Explores the nature of creativity and how to live a more creatively fulfilled life.

- *Surrounded by Idiots* by Thomas Erikson A humorous guide to understanding and working with different personality types in business.

- *The E-Myth Revisited* by Michael E. Gerber A practical handbook on building small businesses with strong foundations.

www.ingramcontent.com/pod-product-compliance
Lightning Source LLC
Chambersburg PA
CBHW051439050726
47593CB00005B/1847